KU-486-010

Communication in Speech

ARTHUR WISE

Lecturer in Speech Education,
University of Leeds

LONGMANS

LONGMANS, GREEN & CO LTD
48 Grosvenor Street, London W1
*Associated companies, branches and representatives
throughout the world*

© *Arthur Wise 1965*
First published 1965
Second impression 1967

PRINTED IN HONG KONG BY THE HONGKONG PRINTING PRESS LTD

EDUCATION TODAY

Communication in Speech

EDUCATION TODAY

Introductory Note

There is an increasing pressure on schools to produce young people with speech that is effective as communication. This pressure will increase greatly in the next few years. At present three university examining boards offer tests in spoken English; they will be joined next year by two other boards. If recommendations in connection with the testing of English in the Certificate of Secondary Education are implemented, we can expect to see very large numbers of young people being tested in the subject in the near future.

We are faced at once with the question: Who is to be responsible in a school for the development of speech? In the absence of a qualified speech-specialist, the answer must inevitably be the classroom teacher without specialist training in the subject. It is for such a teacher that this book is principally intended. It attempts to answer the kind of questions he is likely to ask: 'What does this new subject amount to?', 'What is meant by successful speech?', 'What are the things that can be done in schools to develop skill in oral communication?' The book assumes that the teacher knows his job as a teacher. That is, it assumes that given a clear view of the subject, of the nature of successful speech and of the broad principles involved in speech education, he is able to apply his knowledge of general educational principles to it, and evolve precise class methods in keeping with his own particular needs and circumstances.

The book contains no rhymes and patters. In the first place, there are many books available already that provide these for those who think it necessary to use them. In the second place, exercises of this sort presuppose a clear understanding of the problems they are designed to solve—a presupposition that we cannot make at the moment. Nor does the book contain any anatomical diagrams. These would necessarily be superficial. They are not essential to the argument, and they are in any case available elsewhere.

No book will change the speech of anyone who simply reads it; this book is no exception here. But what it attempts to do is to clarify the attitudes of the non-specialist to the subject, and provide a rational basis on which school work in speech may be founded.

ARTHUR WISE
York, 1964

Contents

Acknowledgements

I am indebted to the following, on whose work I have drawn:
Jack Mitchley and George Hauger in the field of educational
drama, Rosemary Futrell for help in the preparation of Assessment Schemes, and Barbara Claypole and Percy Hitchman for
their work in the testing of Spoken English. I am grateful to
Kenneth Ottaway for insisting that a book of this kind was
necessary. I am particularly grateful to Nan Wise who, as a
very experienced specialist in the field, has helped with the
manuscript at every stage.

I am grateful to the following for permission to reproduce
copyright material:

George Allen & Unwin Ltd and Rand McNally & Company
for material from *The Kon-Tiki Expedition* by Thor
Heyerdahl; The British Broadcasting Corporation for material
from the *B.B.C. Annual Programme, Radio and Television
Broadcasts to Schools and Colleges 1964/65*; Jonathan Cape
Ltd and The Macmillan Company of New York for material
from *Private Angelo* by Eric Linklater, and The Public
Trustee and The Society of Authors for material from
Pygmalion by George Bernard Shaw.

Part One

Speech

I

What is Speech?

Sound

It is customary to begin a book on Speech with that quotation from St John; 'In the beginning was the Word . . .' This may be sound theologically, but it is certainly not the beginning as far as Speech goes. 'In the beginning was Sound', would be far more accurate.

If we hear a broadcast given in a language we have never heard before, the idea that speech is simply a stream of sound and no more, might be a very valid one.

Specific Sounds

But if we listen to the sounds made by a baby lying in its cot, we can be more precise. We can say more than that it is simply 'making sounds'. We may be able to hear something like, 'b-b-b-b' at one moment, and 'p-p-p-p' at another. It is not merely making sounds, it is making *specific* sounds.

Patterns

Suppose we listen to a broadcast in a language that is well-known to us. We hear sound, of course, and we hear a much more complicated version of those specific sounds that were notice-able in the baby. If we wished, we could isolate these sounds from the main stream and imitate them ourselves. We might even describe them a little more accurately by observation or introspection, and say that for this sound the speaker puts his tongue up and for that he rounds his lips.

But we notice something else, something that was not present in the baby; these sounds are arranged in a particular way. There is a pattern to them. There is a coherence about the pattern. If we would write down such a pattern precisely—which we cannot—it might appear something like this:

trayzunionbiznis izcnductid nalmosevricase bymen ovthehigh-isintegriti. . . .

If the broadcast were published in *The Listener,* a different pattern would emerge, a pattern not representing the speech pattern very closely:

Trades Union business is conducted, in almost every case, by men of the highest integrity. . . .

Speech then, is not only sound; it is specific sounds arranged in a particular way.

This pattern is determined by two factors:

1 Those psychological processes taking place inside the speaker, and
2 The grammar of the language he is speaking.

The Listener

All this presupposes that we are there to perceive these patterns and make sense of them. The B.B.C. expects that someone will be listening to the broadcast. It expects from the listener:

1 An ability to hear.
2 An ability to understand the language forms that are being used.
3 An ability to understand the mental processes informing those language forms.
4 An agreement to cooperate by listening.

Voice

The B.B.C. is concerned fundamentally with communication, and if we are concerned with a comprehensive view of speech we must certainly include the idea of its being used to communicate. But for considerable periods the baby in its cot does not appear to be concerned with communication at all. If it is very young it will be concerned only with general sound—the sound of its own voice.

Nevertheless, even at this unskilled level, there are quite a number of things that we can say about this general sound—the Voice:

1 It varies in pitch.
2 It varies in volume.
3 It varies in resonance.
4 Sometimes it appears to be the result of a pure movement activity.
5 Sometimes it appears to carry meaning.
6 It is being used at times to express.
7 It is being used at times to communicate.

In the voice of the adult, all these factors can still be noticed.

Personality

In any sound broadcast, we do not simply interpret the sound complex as meaning, we make a guess as to the sort of person who is speaking. Not only how old he is, but whether he is pleasant or unpleasant, authoritative or tentative. The assessment we make will be almost entirely based on his voice—'the way he sounds'. It will have almost nothing to do with the words he is using.

We may make this assessment unconsciously, but that is beside the point. The conclusions we come to in our assessment of the kind of person a speaker is, are important for us in terms of communication. If a speaker is attacking young people, for instance, it is clearly significant to know whether he himself is young or old. If he is saying that authoritative speech is essential for the politician, it is obviously significant if he himself sounds tentative.

Visual Speech

But speech is more than very complex sound. If we hear the sound-track of a film on the radio, we may be surprised that any director could have allowed the action to be so slow:

'I love you,' says the hero, in a voice resonant with passion.

There is a pause that seems interminable, until at long last the heroine breathes 'I love *you*'.

If we see the film in a cinema, the effect is entirely different. The long and tiresome pause is no longer a meaningless lapse of time. It is an opportunity deliberately created by the director so that the actors can communicate in some other way:

'I love you,' says the hero.

He moves quickly towards her. She puts out a hand to hold him at arm's length. She is not repulsing him entirely, but merely suspending the situation until she has time to assess it. Finally she turns away. He holds her arm and she makes no attempt to free herself. She bites her lower lip. As she turns to face him again, we see that there are tears in her eyes.

'I love *you*,' she says at last.

The sight of the two actors communicating attitudes and feelings in visual terms, gives us essential information.

We cannot say that this has nothing to do with speech. Any comprehensive view of speech must include all those factors which are used by one human being to communicate with another in a living situation. The visual is inextricably bound up with the audible as part of speech. As such, we cannot ignore it.

Speech in Context

If we talk to a friend about recent political developments, we might get this:

FRIEND: What's going to happen?

SELF: Where?

F: Vilibo.

S: What's the Government think it's doing? Damn' fools; Sending troops in like that. . . . Tell you this, they'll not get my vote any more.

F: What else could they've done?

S: UN of course: that's what it's there for.

F: Another beer?

S: Mm.

The same subject, discussed with a casual acquaintance at a social gathering, might sound like this:

ACQUAINTANCE: Bit of trouble in Vilibo, I see.

SELF: Yes. I saw it in the paper.

A: I see we've sent the army in.

S: Mm . . . rather wish we'd taken it to the United Nations first. Course, difficult to know without having all the facts.

A: Of course. . . . I say, let me get you another drink.

S: Well—thanks. Gin and French I think it was. . . .

It might be different again if we are talking formally to a local political gathering:

SELF: I woke this morning to read in the paper that troops had been sent into Vilibo. I cannot imagine a more disastrous move, a move more likely to call down on this country the condemnation of the rest of the world. It may be said that we cannot judge before all the facts are before us. But the only fact that matters is already before us—we are committed to a war involving enormous lines of communication, in an area already on the brink of violent explosion. . . .

These three situations are very different from one another, and so is our speech in each of them. It would be a gross breach of the conventions of decent behaviour to use the speech of passage one in the passage two situation. It could also be a piece of political ineptitude, in that it would not necessarily further our case. The speech in each of the three situations is different, not because our basic beliefs change but because the situations themselves demand an adjustment in the method of

7

communicating those beliefs. The situations are dictating, to a large extent, the type of speech being used.

There will, of course, be many other differences between the speech in one situation and that in another, differences that we cannot represent in print. We shall probably be at our loudest when addressing the political group and at our quietest when chatting to the acquaintance. The range of pitch variation may be at its greatest when talking to the close friend, since we can be more emotionally free in the company of someone who knows us well. We shall perhaps be at our slowest with the group, since we will want every point to make its mark. With the group and with the close friend we shall probably be more visually communicative than with the casual acquaintance.

Speech takes place in a situation and that situation makes certain demands of, and places certain restrictions on, the speech we use. We cannot ask whether a certain type of speech is successful or not, unless we know the purpose for which it is being used and the situation in which it is taking place. Successful speech in one situation, may be useless in another.

What is Speech?

If we are to take a comprehensive view of the subject—a view that will allow us to take educational steps towards producing speech which will be successful for all the purposes for which it is likely to be used by a human being—we must extend the frontiers of the current concept.

The popular view of speech at the moment, is that it is written words turned into sound. It obeys the grammatical rules of written language and, in that sense, lags behind written language rather than being in advance of it. There is a 'correct' speech and an 'incorrect' speech, irrespective of the purposes for which it is being used. Such a view is so removed from the facts as to be quite useless as an educational premise.

Speech is a total psychophysical process involving complex mental and physical activity. We must see it as both communication and non-communication. It is conditioned by the

8

situation in which, and by the purpose for which, it is being used. It has visual aspects which are an integral part of the whole process. We must see it as something frequently involving a listener as well as a speaker. It is seen by the listener as revealing personality, and this revelation has an important effect on the total 'meaning' for that listener. It has little, or nothing at all, to do with written language. It has a grammar of its own, in which such concepts as 'the word' and 'the sentence', essential in written language, have no meaning.

To get a clear view of what we are concerned with, we must begin from the beginning, suspending as far as possible those strong preconceptions we have that arise very largely from our school studies of written language.

2

The Learning Process

The normal child is born with the ability to bring its vocal cords together and make voice. But speech it has to learn. In this sense, voice and speech are different things. Either can exist without the other. Both are essential parts of the complex of sound that a speaker makes.

Broadly speaking, the speech learning process is based on Imitation and Association. The child imitates the sounds about it, then associates with those sounds objects, people, attitudes, feelings, sensations, concepts. This kind of thing might be heard in most households where there is a young child:

> PARENT: This is Mummy and that is Daddy. Can you say 'Daddy'? Daddy—can you? That's Daddy, isn't it, Daddy . . . And Daddy's a big man, isn't he? Isn't Daddy a big man? Daddy. Can you say 'Daddy'? Say 'Daddy', Daddy. . . .
> CHILD: (maybe!) Dad-dad-dad-dad.
> PARENT: What a clever boy. Isn't he a clever boy, Daddy?

But this is too simple an example to demonstrate the process adequately. It suggests that speech is, in essence, isolated words, each with its own associations, built together to form a continuity. Such a view is quite inaccurate. Continuity is not something built up from smaller elements. It is a fundamental of speech. Any attempt to reduce it to something more fundamental will destroy speech.

In speech work with children we need constantly to remind ourselves of the imitative side of this learning process. Suppose, instead of 'Daddy', we have this:

PARENT: That's Duddy, isn'tit? Duddy. . . .

or:

PARENT: Thets Deddy, isn'tit? Deddy. . . .

A child hearing either of these, will say either 'Duddy' or 'Deddy'. The process is inevitable. There is no God-given critical faculty in the child that will tell it that in some English circumstances both these pronunciations will draw forth a certain condemnation. Whatever sound the child is regularly exposed to, it will imitate.

It is necessary to remember, too, that the associative aspect of the process is quite arbitrary. It is learnt. There is nothing God-given that allows a child to know that 'Daddy' is associated by the rest of us with a father. If we wished to do the child a serious disservice, there is nothing in the nature of the process to prevent our saying 'Daddy' to it whilst at the same time waving a frying-pan in front of it. Given time it would associate the sound 'Daddy' with the object that the rest of us associate with 'frying-pan'.

It is still too simple an idea to suggest that the learning process is confined to particular sounds and their associations. What is learned is the total speech activity. We can postulate, on the lines of Adler's 'Family Life Style', a 'Family Speech Style'. We find examples of this, from time to time, when using the telephone:

Hello? Hyde Park seven-two-five-two. . . .

Hello, Mary. John here. About this afternoon . . .

Mary's out, I'm afraid. This is Jean.

Oh, I'm sorry. I thought it was your sister.

Not only does the child learn particular sounds, it learns at what volume to make them in its particular family environment. It learns at what speed to speak, in accordance with the general family speed. It learns what voice quality to produce and what variations of intonation pattern to play. When it is a little older, it learns whether the Family Speech Style permits easy, spontaneous exchanges of speech, or whether it is a 'children should be seen and not heard' Speech Style. Some children are quiet, some are noisy; some are fluent, some are monosyllabic. When we meet their parents it is clear why this is. They have learnt not only particular sounds; they have learnt a total oral process with all its associated social aspects.

The Family Speech Style is not the only Speech Style. Important too is the Speech Style of the area immediately outside the home. Since, in England, speech is so intimately associated with class, we may call this, without being unduly offensive, a Class Speech Style. There is the Speech Style of the classroom and of the school itself. There are, later, Speech Styles of particular professions and particular universities. The Church, the Royal Navy and Balliol College, Oxford, have their own particular Speech Styles. All are *total* Styles, demanding a certain conformity not only to particular sounds, but to volume, speed, voice quality and intonation pattern.

3

Speech as Non-Communication

In education, of necessity, we think of speech very largely as communication.

But suppose we could invade the privacy of the British bathroom at eight o'clock in the morning, and fit a microphone behind the shaving mirror. In some cases we should hear the sounds of fully vocalized speech: 'Wow, that's hot!' 'Blast this razor!' 'Where on earth . . . ?' It would depend on our definition of speech as to whether we regarded this as speech or not. But there would be cases that we would have to regard as speech. Suppose we heard this:

'dum-dum di-dum-dum-dum. . . . Mmmm! . . . Let's see. There's that five-hundred pounds in steel—might fetch three-fifty . . . mm—that's seven hundred with the loot from the Building Society . . . dum dudum dum—wait a bit, wait a bit; didn't Sarah mention some money from Aunt Jenny. . . ? (He opens the bathroom door and shouts) I say, Sarah!'

This is speech. It carries meaning to us in a quite precise way. But it is clearly not meant to communicate. The speaker is using speech for some other purpose; he is using it to consider his financial affairs. As a result of this process involving speech, he reaches a conclusion from which action arises; he opens the bathroom door and calls to his wife. The question of interest to us here is this: would he have seen that the answer to his financial problems might lie with his wife, if it had not been for speech?

Suppose the speaker is a bank manager. He spends some of

his working hours alone in his private office considering financial problems. If we were in a position to watch him closely we might see that even here he has not entirely dispensed with speech. We might see the 'shadow movements' of speech—the slight movements of the Adam's Apple, of the lips, and of the tongue.

In the child the process is much more obvious. If we set the eight-year-old, for example, this problem:

When you walk out of the school and turn left, what is the name of the second street on your right? The process by which it produces an answer will almost certainly be accompanied by the visible movements of speech. We can go a stage further and ask it to solve a similar problem without any of the accompanying speech movements. Its success in inhibiting the movements of speech will be directly related to its difficulty in arriving at a solution. What we have done is denied it access to one of the principal tools by which it carries out this mental activity.

Speech and mental activity are clearly not the same thing here, but they are so involved with each other that they cannot be considered in isolation.

The example of the bank manager may not be typical. We might watch adults and see no observable 'shadow movements' of speech taking place. It would be unwise to conclude definitely from this that no speech processes are taking place below the level at which they could be seen.[1]

There is another aspect of this relationship between speech and mental processes that is concerned, not with the use of the movements of speech for the purposes of *conducting* mental processes, but with the relationship of speech to the *development* of such processes. 'Logical thought,' said Adler, 'would be impossible without speech.'

Luria and Yudovic, in their work with backward twins,[2] discovered that the degree of lack of mental development was

---

[1] Edfeldt, A. W.: *Silent Speech and Silent Reading,* Almqvist and Wiksell, Stockholm.

[2] Luria, A. R., and Yudovitch, F. I.: *Speech and the Development of Mental Processes in the Child.* Staples.

directly related to the degree of lack of speech development. They discovered, too, that where formal speech education took place there was a consequent development of mental processes.

The educational implications are considerable. Where speech education takes place in schools at the moment, it is almost entirely geared to the concept of speech as communication. The case put forward frequently to justify the introduction of speech education in a school, is the vocational one: the teacher, the telephonist, the auctioneer, all speak; our pupils are going into such professions when they leave school; it is therefore part of our job to fit them vocally for such professions. But if speech is essential for the development of mental processes, and used in the carrying out of such processes, it is clearly something of profound educational significance. We should have no difficulty in justifying the active study of speech throughout the educational system, without any reference at all to its communicative aspect.

It is essential to realize that our concern here has been with speech and not with written language. As Ewing points out,[1] a child denied access to spoken language through deafness, shows signs of severe mental retardation. By contrast, there are no signs of lack of satisfactory mental development in populations like that of England in the nineteenth century, for example, which were largely denied access to written language through widespread illiteracy.

Speech as Movement

We can take another view of speech that has nothing to do with communication. We can view it as a highly coordinated system of movement. The simplest sound that we can produce, requires movements of the chest wall, the abdominal wall and the diaphragm. It requires movements of the muscles of the larynx, to bring the vocal cords together at the necessary degree of tension. It requires movements of the jaw, tongue, lips and soft-palate, to form a mouth cavity of the size and shape neces-

[1] Ewing, I. R., and Ewing, A. W. G.: *The Handicap of Deafness.* Longmans.

sary for the production of the particular sound at which we are aiming. Any movement imprecision or discoordination in this process, will result in a different sound from the one we are trying to produce.

This view of speech is important in speech education, since any change in speech requires a change in those movements producing speech. One sound can be changed to another only by a teacher who knows these three things:

i   The movements involved in making the present sound.

ii   The movements involved in making the new sound.

iii   The principles involved in changing one movement habit to another.

4
Speech as Communication

Speech is used for purposes which have nothing to do with communication, but undoubtedly our principal concern in education is with speech that is used to communicate.

We might begin by defining communication as far as it concerns speech, as 'the passing of information from one person to another, or group of others, by means of sound'.

But this is not sufficient. Communication requires not only a speaker to pass information but a listener who is willing and able to receive it.

To make a person assume the role of listener we must establish a relationship with him. The creation of this relationship must precede the passage of information since without it we can speak forever and never communicate. Suppose we sit down at the breakfast table and say:

'Pass the marmalade, please.'

If there are a number of people at the table, nothing might happen. It is not that we have not been heard, but that we have not created a listener who will translate our request into action. It will be quite different if we create our listener first:

'Mary.'
'Mm?'
'Pass the marmalade, please.'

'Mary' is not passing information to anyone. It is simply a call by which we may establish the necessary relationship with someone who is sitting near the marmalade. We could establish the relationship equally well by a raising of the eyebrows or a smile. The technical device we use is not important; the relationship itself is vital.

The word 'information' needs a little elaboration. We may think of it simply as a number of facts. But to imagine that this is all that is implied by the word, is to suggest that all that is carried on the railways are parcels. In the case of a bomb being sent by rail to a politician, we might say that 'hatred' is carried by rail. We should see 'information' in this context as including anything, facts, feeling, attitudes, that can be passed from one person to another in terms of speech.

Communication, as we have seen, requires two people; someone to pass information and someone prepared to receive it. John passes information to Edward who, as a cooperative listener receives it. But suppose Edward, though quite prepared to be a cooperative listener, is a little hard of hearing:

JOHN: You're standing on my foot.
EDWARD: Eh?
JOHN: I say you're standing on my foot.
EDWARD: Speak up.
JOHN: You're standing on my foot!
EDWARD: Oh . . . sorry!

This is not a simple one-way process. John is passing information to Edward, but Edward is also passing information back to John. In the light of this 'response information', John passes the initial information in a slightly altered form. This alteration in form, altered either in terms of the words used, or the speed, or the volume, is the direct result of the 'response information' that Edward has passed back along the contact that has been established between them.

This 'response information' need not be given in speech terms. It can be visual:

JOHN: (*shouting above the clatter of machinery*) You're standing on my foot.
EDWARD: (*cups his hand round his ear*)
JOHN: My foot!
EDWARD: Oh . . . sorry!

18

So we can say these things about speech as communication:

i   Communication presupposes a relationship between two or more people.

ii   Communication has little to do with words, and far more with the attitude of one human being to another.

iii   Communication is the passing of information, in the widest sense, through this relationship.

iv   Communication is not a one-way process from speaker to listener. It is a process that allows the passage of 'primary information' in one direction, and 'response information' in the opposite direction.

v   The method of passing the primary information, though not necessarily the information itself, is conditioned by the response information that a speaker receives.

vi   This response information may be given in nonvocal terms.

5
Types of Communication

Through the relationship between speaker and listener, a complex of information can be passed. It is this complex that gives the listener his total view of what is meant. Some of the detailed pieces of information in this complex may be in conflict with one another; they may be saying different things to the listener. To arrive at his sense of total meaning, the listener must balance one conflicting piece of information with another and come to a conclusion regarding the validity of each.

The best example of uncomplicated communication in speech terms, is perhaps the radio newsreader. He is concerned with passing to a cooperative listener factual information in as dispassionate a way as possible. In the successful newsreader, only one other piece of information reaches us apart from the particular information he is passing; we can tell his sex from his voice.

The uncomplicated communication of the radio newsreader is rare. As an example of a more typical communicative act, we can consider the politician on his platform saying something along these lines:

'The government has said that it is now prepared to consider some form of limited and controlled disarmament. If other countries are prepared to reduce expenditure on arms by a certain percentage, the government of this country will do the same.

'There's not a person here tonight who won't be relieved

by the news—until he remembers that in February of last year the same government spokesman said exactly the same thing. Why should we believe the government's any more in earnest now than it was then? . . .'

What is he communicating here? When he was preparing his speech what information did he intend to pass to the listeners? He intended to pass a simple piece of information in the same way as the newsreader: 'The government has said that it is now prepared to consider some form of limited and controlled disarmament.' But he intended to do more; he intended to comment on the government's decision in a way that would leave a listener in no doubt about the speaker's attitude to it. 'The government is prepared to consider—but!'

This additional information—the speaker's attitude to the facts—is a common aspect of oral communication. It may be conveyed in terms of words, as in the case of our example, or it may be conveyed by the way in which he speaks the facts. Both the facts and the comment on them may be given at the same time. 'The government has said that it is now prepared to consider some form of limited and controlled disarmament,' can be a simple statement of fact, or it can contain, in the way it is said, the meaning, 'at long last it's made a decision that's been obvious to everyone else for years'.

Both these aspects of communication we may regard as 'intentional', in the sense that it was the speaker's conscious and planned intention to produce them.

But if we regard communication as information passed from one person to another through a preestablished relationship, we cannot ignore that information that reaches the listener without the speaker's being aware of it. Suppose the speaker's comment on the facts is accompanied by a sneer. Not only is he telling us what he thinks of the facts, but he is telling us, presumably unintentionally, something about himself as a person. This information which will be 'unintentional' on his part, is highly significant to a listener. A listener may approve of the speaker's comment on the facts, whilst not approving of the speaker himself. The listener must balance these opposing considerations against one another before he can come to any final conclusion regarding his total attitude to all the information that has been given to him.

Voice as Communication

Words can carry meaning. They can be used to communicate. 'No' means an unequivocal negative.

PETER: *(on the high diving board)* Are you frightened?
JOHN: No.

There is nothing here to lead us to believe that John means anything more than 'No, I'm not frightened.'

But, as we have seen, other things beside the particular words that a speaker uses, carry meaning to a listener. One of these things is 'voice'. On paper that 'No' is unequivocal. But a little personal experiment will show that it can be spoken in such a way as to mean precisely the opposite. It is not that the 'No' actually changes into 'Yes', but that it is accompanied by some additional information not communicated in terms of words, that stoutly contradicts it. We might represent it on paper like this:

JOHN: No (I'm terrified!)

This conflicting information is communicated in terms of the tune John plays on his voice, by the volume at which he speaks, by the slight tremble in his voice, by the long pause before he replies to Peter's question. It is communicated by factors in the whole complex sound that John makes, that have nothing to do with that word 'No'.

Peter's response to this will depend on the strength of the conflicting information. If it simply throws doubt on the unequivocal nature of that 'No', then we might get this:

PETER: Are you scared?
JOHN: No.
PETER: I thought you wanted to dive from here.
JOHN: I do.
PETER: You might sound a bit more sure about it.

If the conflicting information is stronger, then we will get this:

PETER: Are you scared?
JOHN: No.
PETER: You go back and wait for me at the bottom.
JOHN: But I—
PETER: Go on.

In the case of a real conflict between what the word is saying and what the voice is saying, Peter has no hesitation in deciding which of the two is more accurately reflecting what is going on inside John. It is the word that he discounts and the voice that he believes.

Visual Communication

On the radio a speaker must make do with his voice and speech. But the radio is not a typical communication medium. The teacher, the politician, the lawyer, the baby, can usually be seen as well as heard, and this fact is significant to a listener.

Visual communication, arising out of movement, is fundamental to the theatre. In Mime, the performers have access to no other tool of communication but the visual. The fact that Mime has developed into an autonomous theatrical form, is an indication of the communicative subtleties that are possible in terms of sight alone. We reach the limitations of Mime, and therefore of the visual, only when we need to pass detailed and often quite superficial pieces of information.

Essentially the difference between words and movement, as aspects of the total communicative process, is this: words tell us facts; movement shows us facts in action. A person may say 'I am unhappy', and be nothing of the sort. The words stand between the listener and the object to which they refer. But for a person to show himself as unhappy, he must first create the unhappy person to show. He cannot show what does not exist. It is for this reason that listeners attach fundamental importance to what they see; they know that it reflects what exists. In the case of a conflict between what the words are saying and the information that is reaching the listener in visual terms, it is the words that he will discard.

6

Voice and Personality

It is clear that besides all the other things a listener gets from a particular speaker, he gets a total impression of what that speaker is like as a person. This total personality reading that the listener makes, is highly significant for him. Everything that the speaker says in words is measured against it.

A speaker might be saying these words:

> 'In my opinion, wrestling should be taught in all boys' schools. It is the most masculine of all male sports. It teaches agility and poise on the physical side, and on the character-building side it teaches courage, endurance and ability to take punishment in a sportsmanlike way.
>
> 'It is often argued that professional wrestling is a fake; that fights are arranged beforehand. But anyone who has been a professional wrestler, as I have, will know that the blood trickling from his nose as the result of a properly delivered forearm smash, is very real blood. . . .'

In this case, the listener's impression of the speaker as a person is crucial. For complete success, the speaker must fall as a person within the listener's concept of what a professional wrestler is like.

If the speaker is tall, with broad shoulders and mangled ears and a deep, resonant voice, the listener may be convinced.

But suppose the speaker has a voice that is 'thin' and 'reedy'. This could be so pronounced as to make the listener associate it with 'effeminacy'. If this is the personality impression the listener forms, he might have difficulty in restraining his

24

7

Conversational Situations

A person uses speech for a variety of purposes and in a variety of situations. We cannot ask the question, 'Is this good speech?' unless we know the purpose for which it is being used, and understand the situation in which it is taking place.

Speech which is successful in one situation, may be quite useless in another. Successful speech over the coffee table is useless in the classroom. Successful speech in the classroom is useless in the theatre. Successful speech in the theatre is useless in the committee-room. So there are many types of successful speech, all of them dependent on purpose and situation. All these types differ from one another in every way: not only do they differ in vocabulary, but in speed, in voice quality, in articulatory precision, in intonation pattern and in volume.

We can make a very broad division of the situations in which speech takes place for communication purposes, on the basis of whether that speech is related to conversation or not. The conversational situation is the one in which a human being first experiences speech and the one in which his own speech is learnt.

There are certain principles governing this situation, that mark it off from those situations which we cannot regard as being conversational.

Numbers

The conversational situation is severely restricted as far as the number of people who can take part in it goes. The smallest number of people necessary for conversation is two. The largest number who can take part in a speech situation that we can still regard as genuinely conversational, is probably five or six. Beyond that number, the situation begins to change. It begins to take on characteristics that we can no longer regard as being strictly conversational.

Unpredictable

The development of conversation is unpredictable. It might begin with one topic, pass through a number of others, and finish at last with a topic that appears quite unrelated to the first. Internal processes in the mind of one person might be stirred; such processes might change the development entirely. Equally, the development might be altered by the intrusion of some external factor.

Experimental

Conversation is experimental. It allows us to try out new ideas, at times quite outrageous ones, without feeling that we are going to be held absolutely responsible for everything we say. Some of our statements in conversation are no more than try-outs in public of ideas that we are in the process of formulating. Conversation gives us the opportunity of testing the validity of new ideas by the reactions of others, without being held responsible for them. For example:

> JAMES: This road-accident business wants looking into, you know.
> HENRY: Half the drivers in this country are drunks.
> EDWARD: Bosh!
> HENRY: Well—you know what I mean. . . .

Henry doesn't feel that Edward has called upon him to justify his statement. He can shrug it off because conversation allows such statements and does not take them very seriously.

Similar experiments are possible in conversation with new words which are just beginning to be absorbed into a person's vocabulary. The words can be tried out in conversation; their exact meaning can be tested by the effect they produce on the listener.

Pressures

Conversation does not exert strong pressures on us to conform to certain rigid standards of speech. In most true conversational situations, we are not constantly on the lookout lest we drop an 'h', or break some treasured law of the grammar of written language, or reveal ourselves as having a pronunciation which might be regarded in certain circles as socially unacceptable.

In this sense, conversation is the freest speech situation.

Voluntary

We can leave a conversational situation more or less at will:

HENRY: I told him straight; I said, 'Since you took over this section there's been nothing but trouble.'
JAMES: So what did he say?
HENRY: Oh, he got on his high horse; he said, 'Jenkins,' he said, 'what you call trouble, I call discipline.'
JAMES: So what did you say?
HENRY: What did *I* say? I told him a thing or two. I said, 'Mr Fryer,' I said, 'what you call discipline is going to close these works. Nobody's going to stand . . .'
JAMES: (*looking at his watch*) Bless me, Henry. Is that the time? I said I'd pick up Jenny at half-past: it's nearly a quarter to. . . .

And James is free to turn and walk away.

The Wedding-Guest in Coleridge's *Ancient Mariner*, is not in a conversational situation, if for no other reason than that he is unable to leave when he wishes:

> The Wedding-Guest he beat his breast,
> Yet he cannot choose but hear.

The lack of choice makes the situation non-conversational within our definition of conversation.

Acoustics

It is difficult to converse with a friend when standing at the foot of an alpine waterfall, without making some adjustment of volume. But for most conversations external acoustics do not have to be taken into consideration. Physical conditions that would make non-conversational speech extremely difficult, hardly affect conversation with a friend a mere two feet away, at all.

This is the situation—conversation—in which a child learns to speak. It is the only situation in which he has any speech skill when he first enters school. Denied any direct experience outside this situation, it will remain the only one in which he has any speech skill when he leaves school.

8

Non-Conversational Situations

If we regard the Conversational Situation as that in which a human being *learns* to speak, then we might regard the Non-conversational Situation as being that in which many people *function* in speech in adult life. The lawyer has learnt to speak in the intimate, conversational situation of the family. But when he addresses the jury with the words, 'My learned friend has told you that . . .', he would be rash to think that he was functioning in an extended form of conversation.

There is a tendency to think of all speech situations as being merely extensions of the conversational one. It would be safer to regard professional situations as differing fundamentally from conversation. We might see how different the two situations are, if we examine in some detail the nature of a speech situation with which we are all familiar: the teaching situation. Teaching requires a special speech skill that conversation can never teach.

Status

When a teacher opens the door of a classroom, he is in a special position. His status is not the same as that of anyone else in the class.

> GEORGE: It's mine.
> JOHN: No it isn't.
> GEORGE: I bought it.
> JOHN: No you didn't.
> ERIC: I saw him.

ALFRED: So did I.

JOHN: No you didn't.

GEORGE: I'll hit you.

JOHN: No you won't.

(*The door opens.*)

ERIC: Hey—ssh! It's teacher.

Numbers

The teacher, if he is fortunate, may face a group of twenty-five children each day. If he is less fortunate, the number may be in excess of forty. As we have seen, these are numbers far in excess of those that characterize conversation.

A headmaster might talk for a few moments each morning in assembly, to a thousand boys. A university teacher may talk for fifty minutes to a group of two hundred students. Such numbers bear no relationship at all to those involved in conversation.

Predictability

In contrast to conversation, the degree of predictability in teaching is very high. However casual a particular piece of teaching may appear to an outsider, there is nevertheless a predictability about it that is quite foreign to the conversational situation. A teacher's conduct of the class may appear to be very informal and he may encourage a good deal of discussion, but it will be discussion related to his preconceived ideas. For example:

TEACHER: Well now, what sort of things do you think we'd have seen if we'd been present at one of the performances of a tragedy in ancient Greece? Mm? Jones—what about you? Do you know?

JONES: Sir: there was a production of *Lysistrata* on television on Monday.

TEACHER: Mm? (*meaning*: It doesn't sound very relevant, but tell me a bit more before I decide.)

JONES: Sir, it was about some women who decided to stop a war that the men were fighting, and . . .

TEACHER: No (*meaning:* If I let this go on it will lead us outside the framework I've laid down for this class.) That shows us what it's like on television, not what it must have been like to the first audience who saw it. . . . In any case, *Lysistrata's* a comedy. Andrews, what about you. . . ?

This preconceived framework is characteristic of many non-conversational situations. It is never a characteristic of conversation.

Experimental

In conversation we can try out new ideas for our own benefit. For the class, this experimental factor is still operative. The child is at liberty to some extent to try out a new idea that has just occurred to him. It can be tested against the teacher's greater knowledge and experience, and either discarded or retained in the light of the teacher's reaction to it.

But for the teacher himself there is room for little such experiment whilst he is actually in the process of teaching. The statement, 'Half the drivers in this country are drunks', is not the kind of statement that we associate with the classroom. This is not because the statement itself is false, but because spoken by a teacher seriously in a classroom, it carries an authority that it does not deserve.

Pressures

We have seen in conversation that the pressure on a person to speak according to certain standards of acceptability, is not very strong. This is not true in the classroom. The image of what a teacher should be is closely tied to speech. 'Not the sort of speech one expects from a teacher', is a not-uncommon comment made by supervisors of student teachers. There is a constant pressure on the teacher to conform in speech to the concept of what a teacher should be.

Speech is learnt by imitation. The teacher knows that whether he likes it or not he cannot avoid being used by the children he teaches as a 'speech model' who will be imitated in a general sense. He is under constant pressure to produce speech worthy of such imitation.

Non-voluntary

In this country, a child must be in full-time attendance at a school between the ages of five and fifteen. If he is not, investigations are made to establish why.

The teacher is in a similar position. However much he may feel that he could be doing something else much more useful, he is held in the situation by its terms of reference.

This lack of freedom is characteristic of many non-conversational situations, both for the listener and the speaker. It is possible to stay away from church at will, but once inside it is impossible to leave during the progress of a service without some substantial reason. In church, social pressures operate to keep us there until the proceedings have run their course.

Acoustics

The speech of a teacher takes place inside a classroom. Sound produced inside the classroom is affected by the classroom's physical structure. Most classrooms, particularly in older schools, tend to reflect rather than absorb sound. This 'echo' effect can so distort speech that would be entirely successful in conversation, as to make it incomprehensible to listeners sitting at a distance from the speaker. In many teaching situations, the teacher has to recognize this fact and make conscious speech adjustments to overcome it.

There are classrooms which, kind enough to the speech of the teacher in themselves, are constructed alongside a railway line, or a busy traffic route. Others open directly into a central hall which is used throughout the day for physical education and games. This noise, coming into the classroom from outside, forms a part of the total acoustic situation in which the teacher has to speak.

These problems arising from external acoustic conditions are common to many non-conversational situations. The preacher, the actor, the auctioneer and the drill sergeant, all face situations which are more difficult than that of the teacher. All must make considerable speech adjustments if they are to be understood.

Time

The teacher is expected to speak for long periods. This time factor is important. Possible strain of the vocal apparatus is negligible in conversation. It is far from negligible in teaching. One of the important factors determining the degree of such strain, is the need to produce audible sound for long periods.

The time factor is common to many other non-conversational situations. The lawyer, the preacher, the politician, are called upon as part of their professional activities to produce voice and speech in difficult circumstances for long periods.

These facts suggest that teaching and conversation are activities that differ from one another in an almost fundamental way. Wide experience in conversation will not necessarily produce that different type of speech essential for good teaching. To do this a person must be given training and experience in non-conversational speech.

If we are concerned with producing fully developed human beings, fitted to take their place in a society which increasingly demands an ability to communicate orally in situations wider than that of a small circle of friends and relations, we must see that children have sufficient experience of the problems of non-conversational situations to enable them to handle such situations with at least the ease and skill they frequently show in conversation.

9

What is Successful Speech?

We can say, quite simply, that successful speech is that which fulfils all the demands being made upon it. These demands, as we have seen, are for speech as communication in both conversational and non-conversational situations, together with speech for non-communicative purposes.

But this is not very helpful if our concern is to try educationally to change unsuccessful speech into speech which is successful. We will need to know at what points a particular child's speech is unsuccessful, so that we may develop those points in particular. We will need to know, too, how important these particular points are in the total sound complex. We will need a certain sense of priorities. And since we have direct access to a child's speech only when it is being used for communicative purposes, we need to consider the points which determine whether it is successful or not as communication.

Audibility

If any one aspect of the total communicative act has an overriding importance, it is the one of audibility. Sufficient noise is an absolute prerequisite of speech communication. Technically it is dependent upon a speaker's ability to bring together the vocal cords and pass a sufficient volume of air between them in a given space of time. Psychologically, it is dependent on many other things, some of which we shall need to look at when we consider how speech might be changed.

Intelligibility

But mere volume of sound, although essential, is scarcely sufficient for successful speech communication.

The intelligibility of speech, at the technical level at which we are considering it here, is dependent on the ability of a speaker to make clear distinctions between one sound and the next. This ability depends on the speed and accuracy with which he can move his organs of articulation.

Flexibility

We can require of a speaker a flexibility in the use of his mechanism that will allow it to respond automatically to whatever feelings and attitudes he wishes to communicate. If he is anxious to communicate a feeling of righteous anger, for example, his mechanism should be sufficiently flexible to give to a listener those clues that will leave him in no doubt as to the speaker's feelings.

Unobtrusive

If communication is our principal concern, anything that interferes with its immediacy is unsatisfactory. Some people have voice and speech which is described as ugly; others have voice and speech that is described as beautiful. Both are unsatisfactory for communication purposes if these qualities distract the attention of the listener from the material that is being communicated.

Oral communication does not demand voice and speech that is beautiful. It demands voice and speech that does its job of transmitting a message in the most unobtrusive way.

Pronunciation

MAVIS: John's mummy says 'gless'.

MUMMY: Yes, dear, I know John's mummy says 'gless'. But we don't say 'gless', do we? We say 'glahss'. You can say 'glahss', can't you, darling?

37

MAVIS: Glahss.
MUMMY: That's a clever girl. . . .

Out of the whole oral communication complex, pronunciation is the aspect that has come in for most public attention. Bernard Shaw's play *Pygmalion* is sustained by the very naïve view that speech is pronunciation and nothing else:

THE SARCASTIC BYSTANDER: I can tell where you come from. You come from Anwell. Go back there.
THE NOTE TAKER: (*helpfully*) *H*anwell.
THE SARCASTIC BYSTANDER: (*affecting great distinction of speech*) Thenk you, teacher. Haw haw! So long (*he touches his hat with mock respect and strolls off*). (Act I, *Pygmalion*.)

This popular view of pronunciation may be summarized like this:

i   Speech *is* pronunciation.
ii   Aesthetic judgments may be made about pronunciation. Some pronunciations of a sound are ugly, others are not. 'u', in some northern pronunciations of 'butter', is an ugly sound. 'u', in a word like 'put', is not.
iii   Social judgments can be made about pronunciation. Some speech is 'working class', some speech is 'vulgar':
THE NOTE TAKER: . . . This is an age of upstarts. Men begin in Kentish Town with £80 a year, and end in Park Lane with a hundred thousand. They want to drop Kentish Town; but they give themselves away every time they open their mouths. Now I can teach them—— (Act I, *Pygmalion*.)
iv   Moral judgments can be made about pronunciation. The Sarcastic Bystander's 'Anwell' is lazy. It is bad pronunciation. 'Hanwell' is good pronunciation. The Sarcastic Bystander could say 'Hanwell' if he made the effort. He persists in saying 'Anwell' because he is a slipshod person. Bad pronunciation reflects a defect of character.

Most of these views of pronunciation will not stand up to any rational scrutiny. If we explore the common comment, 'his speech is vulgar', we shall find in all probability that what the commentator is really saying is this: 'The background that I associate with this person's speech, is one of poverty, dirt and meanness. My own upbringing has taught me to regard such a background as "vulgar".' This may be a fair or unfair sociological comment, but it has little to do with speech. If we remember that speech is not a gift from God, but something that is learned by imitation of the speech around one, we will see that the pronunciation 'Anwell', is not an indication of that personality flaw suggested by the word 'laziness'. If a person's pronunciation bears the marks of speech from a particular geographical area or economic background, it is because that person has imitated speech models from that area or with that background. We need constantly to remind ourselves, in considering pronunciation, that a person will inevitably imitate those sounds that surround him during the process of his learning to speak. If a member of the Royal Family were brought up surrounded by the speech of Huddersfield, for example, that member would *inevitably* speak the speech of Huddersfield.

But the fact that these widely held views on pronunciation do not bear rational scrutiny, is not sufficient reason for us to dismiss them as quite unimportant. Rightly or wrongly, they exist. Rightly or wrongly, they are brought to bear by very many people in the process of making judgments on speech, and therefore on the speaker as the person behind that speech. Such judgments have at times a very significant effect on communication; they are judgments that are unlikely to disappear in the foreseeable future. We cannot tell our school-leaver to ignore such judgments entirely, because they are based on a complete misunderstanding of the nature of speech. They are judgments which can have a profound effect on the course of his life, and we should make him at least aware of this.

It is difficult to make a statement about the standards that we can apply to the pronunciation of the school-leaver, that are both real standards and standards that will stand up to rational scrutiny. If we could say that a particular type of local pronunciation was universally execrated, however strongly we disagreed with the views implied by that execration, we should at least have some basis from which to offer reasonable advice to a school-leaver:

> 'I can see nothing wrong with your pronunciation myself. Unfortunately, most people are not as enlightened in this matter as I am. You happen to have a pronunciation that every English speaker detests. If I were you I'd think of changing it.'

Unfortunately, we are in no such happy position. Pronunciation which is roundly denigrated in Newcastle, may be thought positively attractive in Portsmouth. If we consider this fact for a moment, we begin to see the glimmering of a pattern. It is this: the place where a particular local pronunciation is most strongly denigrated is the place of its origin. Leeds speech seems most strongly to be denigrated in Leeds, Birmingham speech in Birmingham, London speech in London. We shall see a reason for this if we remember that most comments on pronunciation are not so much speech comments as sociological comments. They are not comments on the speech itself, but on the background out of which that speech springs. A person brought up in Liverpool knows the background that has produced a certain type of Liverpool speech. The background, and the speech it produces, coalesce. If he dislikes the background he dislikes the speech that symbolizes it for him. For the Londoner, faced with the speech of Liverpool, no such connection exists. He hears the speech, but he has no close personal knowledge of the background which has produced it. His comments on Liverpool speech are more reasonable, because they are comments on the speech alone and not on the background it symbolizes.

The attitude of many Englishmen to the speech of their own area, is quite unreal. It is possible to hear a person strongly condemning the speech of his own area that is entirely successful as communication, whilst at the same time praising the totally unsuccessful spoken English of a Frenchman from the gutters of Marseilles. The reason is simple; the Englishman knows his own backstreets and the speech that springs from them, but he has no knowledge of the gutters of Marseilles. It would almost seem that the best advice we can give to the school-leaver is to leave his pronunciation alone and live as far away from home as possible.

We must, of course, distinguish quite clearly between a pronunciation which simply reflects a particular area or background, and articulation which is so imprecise as to be difficult to understand. The two are not necessarily related. It is quite common for a person to have a pronunciation which is socially frowned on and at the same time have articulation so imprecise that he is difficult to understand. But it is quite as common for a person to have a type of spoken English that is entirely socially acceptable and yet wellnigh incomprehensible.

Perhaps the only reasonable demand we can make concerning pronunciation, is to say that if a person's pronunciation is so markedly of a particular small locality as to be difficult to understand by a listener speaking the same language then, assuming that the speaker wishes to communicate with this particular listener, he will have to adjust his pronunciation. This is a defensible position to take up as regards pronunciation, since it is a reapplication of the standard of communication that we have been concerned with throughout.

But it is such a wide view that it is perhaps not very useful. There may be many children we encounter whose pronunciation is not seriously detrimental to reasonable communication, but which, for one reason or another, we feel should be changed in some way. In our later considerations we shall have to see what is really involved in making changes of pronunciation.

Vocal Health

The world in which we find ourselves, is so highly vocal, that we tend to forget that a person may live without ever being able to speak. Speech is essential for life in human society, but it is not vital for life itself.

All the mechanism used in the process of communication through speech, is designed for purposes which have nothing to do with speech. The vital function of breathing, is the oxygenation of the blood. A failure of breathing at this level will result in death. A secondary aspect of breathing is that it can be used as part of the speech process. A failure at this level will result in no more than a lack of sound. The vital function of the vocal cords is the closure of the upper end of the respiratory tract, so that such essential functions as defaecation may take place. The cords can also be used for the production of voice, but this is a secondary, and non-vital function.

Voice and speech are produced by the movements of live tissue, designed principally for some other and more important purpose. The production of voice and speech in a way that ignores the limitations of such tissue will result inevitably in its damage. 'Clergyman's Sore Throat' and 'Teacher's Sore Throat', are terms that are widely used to classify that type of laryngitis whose cause is the habitual misuse of vocal tissue.[1]

We can reasonably demand, then, that the school leaver should have an ability to produce voice and speech for purposes of communication, in such a way that the flesh and blood with which he is working is not strained beyond endurance.

The Processes Behind Speech

On the face of it, these appear to be purely technical demands. The comments on Audibility might suggest that any lack of success can be changed by simply passing more breath through the closed vocal cords. The comments on Intelligibility might suggest that to make a person clearly understood, demands only a greater precision of articulatory movements.

This mechanistic view might have validity to the observer, but to the speaker himself it is totally inadequate. What he is principally concerned with are those processes behind his speech—the information, the feelings, the attitudes he is trying to pass to someone else. So for successful speech communication we can demand two things which are so intimately related to one another as to be inseparable:

    i A well-organized and fluent psychological process inside the speaker.

---

[1] McCallum: 'Chronic Laryngitis', *Speech*, Vol. 18, No. 2.

ii   A technical ability to externalize that process in terms of sound.

The development of both these processes to the level of skill that we can require of the school-leaver, is almost entirely dependent on what opportunities the child has been given for practice and experience in speech work throughout his school life.

Part Two

Speech in School

I

Speech and Education

LADY BRACKNELL: . . . I do not approve of anything that tampers with natural ignorance. . . .

Unlike Lady Bracknell, most people not only approve of tampering with natural ignorance but positively encourage it. We might think that many of them would go so far as to define education itself as 'a praiseworthy tampering with natural ignorance'.

In educational practice, we no longer restrict ourselves to those subjects which can be learnt, as opposed to those which are innate and God-given. Movement is an ability with which all normal children are born, yet we have no doubt that educational processes can help to develop it in a way that the hit-and-miss process of pure experience cannot. It seems increasingly to be the case, too, that sex, that most God-given of all activities, is regarded as susceptible to the processes of education.

But in its attitude to speech, education has tended to echo Lady Bracknell's words. Until very recently, education has avoided tampering with natural ignorance as regards any widespread attempt to develop speech by established educational processes. Three attitudes seem to have prompted this avoidance of organized speech work in education:

   i   The belief that, since the child can speak when we first meet him, there is nothing for education to do.

   ii   The belief that speech is not a skill that is susceptible to normal educational procedures.

iii   The belief that any attempt to educate speech will result in speech that is 'unnatural'.

These three views require some detailed consideration.

Speech Education as Unnecessary

The normal child can speak when we first meet him. But speech is required by the school-leaver for purposes that are concerned with much more complicated communication than that of conversation with parents or close friends. He requires, too, speech which is efficient for very much more sophisticated mental processes. A denial of such speech is a denial of access to human society. At the moment, the speech of most school-leavers is barely sufficient for either of these needs. Their skill —or lack of it—in speech, is the result of fortunate or unfortunate trial-and-error experience. Not only their speech-skill, but their attitudes to speech, are the result of such haphazard experience. These attitudes can seriously affect their contact with other human beings.

Some speech education process is vital if we are to make sure of three factors:

i   A speech-ability that will allow the school-leaver to receive and transmit information in those complex situations with which adult society will surround him.

ii   A speech-ability that will allow the continued development and conduct of those mental processes that are entirely dependent on speech.

iii   A system of attitudes to speech, and those processes that lie behind speech, that will stand up to rational investigation.

A child comes to school with a particular sex and with an ability to move. It is now established that neither of these facts is sufficient to make sex education and physical education unnecessary in schools. We recognize that a child's movement ability will not be developed very far without some educational attention. We recognize, too, that pure trial-and-error experience is not sufficient to guarantee the reasonable development of healthy sex attitudes. We should recognize also that pure trial-and-error experience of speech is by no means enough to ensure in the school-leaver an ability to handle speech with that proficiency that a complex human society requires. Successful speech development requires full-scale educational intervention.

Speech Not Susceptible to Educational Procedures

The view that speech is something that cannot be educated, implies that it is God-given and fixed. Like the shape of the face or the size of the foot, there is little that education can do to alter it.

Such a view is quite wrong. We have seen that no child, normal or abnormal, is born with the ability to speak. Left outside society, it would never speak. The fact that it can speak when it first enters school, is an indication of the fact that it has already been through some educational process in which it has learned to speak. This educational process has been conducted very largely by parents, whose own speech was produced by the same process. Parents may be kind or unkind, broadminded or narrowminded, but generally they cannot be regarded as educationally skilled merely by virtue of being parents.

The educational process that has taught the child to speak before it reaches school, was unsystematic and haphazard. It was based on beliefs about the nature of speech which in most cases are little more than gross personal prejudices. It is no more than sheer accident if the speech that has resulted from it is entirely successful for the purpose for which it will eventually be required. It would be the negation of all educational belief to argue that the application of skilled educational procedures to the process of speech development would not be an immeasurable improvement on the present process.

Educated Speech is 'Unnatural' Speech

The view that speech that has been through some direct educational process is 'unnatural', is widely held. There is a certain historical justification for such a view. Until recently most speech education fell into one of two categories:

i The education of the actor's speech for particular theatrical purposes.

ii The direct application of the methods and aims of actor-training, to the training of children who would never see the inside of a theatre.

The result was the production of speech designed for specialized use in the theatre. Such speech, used for other purposes, struck the listener as being 'unnatural' and 'affected'. From this the listener drew the inaccurate conclusion that *any* educational interference with speech made it 'unnatural'. What in fact was at fault was not the educational process; that had been all too successful. It had been the aim that was wrong, the intention to produce speech designed for the theatre which was in fact to be used in entirely non-theatrical circumstances. The speech of the paradeground sounds no less 'unnatural' in the drawing-room. The speech of the cathedral sermon sounds no less 'affected' at a cocktail party.

The word 'natural', as applied to speech, suggests that there is a type of speech 'as nature intended it'. But nature never intended speech at all. If there is any 'natural' function of the lungs, it is the oxygenation of the blood. To use them for the purpose of speaking *Hamlet* soliloquies or ordering groceries on the telephone is entirely 'unnatural'. In this sense all speech is 'unnatural'. When we complain that a person's speech is 'unnatural', we are not really complaining that it is not 'in accordance with nature', but that it is being used in such a way that it draws attention to itself to the detriment of the material that the speaker is trying to communicate. If such speech is the outcome of deliberate educational effort, what is at fault is not the principle of speech education in general, but that particular educational process through which that particular speaker has passed. Faced with 'unnatural' movement, we no longer feel justified in condemning physical education. We condemn only the incompetence of one particular physical educationist. We should restrict ourselves to a similar view, when faced by 'unnatural' speech which has been produced by an incompetent speech educational process.

In summarizing our views on Speech and Education we can make the following points:

i   Speech can be developed by known educational processes.

ii   Speech that has been through no educational process, remains restricted to those situations and purposes limited by experience.

iii   All speech is 'unnatural'.

iv   Any speech education process must take into consideration the purposes for which speech is to be used.

v   Any speech education process must be based on a clear view of what the endproduct is to be like.

vi   Since speech is available in the classroom only in terms of communication, it is at successful communication that speech education should be primarily aimed.

2

What Factors in a School Improve Speech?

From 1957 to 1964, the School Examination Board of the University of Durham conducted tests in Spoken English. Candidates from some schools were found to be consistently good; candidates from others were found to be consistently poor. Since the tests were conducted by examiners who visited these schools, it was possible to draw certain conclusions to account for these extremes of achievement.

The Timetable

A visitor to a school where the level of speech development is high, may be surprised to see from the timetable in the headmaster's study that there are no periods marked 'Speech Education'. He may be still more surprised to find 'Speech Education' appearing frequently on the timetable of a school where the level of speech development is low.

He will be unwise to conclude that classes in Speech Education produce a low level of speech. Closer investigation may show him that in the good speech school, all the classes timetabled as 'English (Drama)' are conducted in oral terms. In a poor speech school he may find all the classes under the heading of 'Speech Education' are confined to practising in isolation the vowels of southern standard English.

The School Play

In both schools the visitor may find that plays are performed in the hall twice a year.

In the good speech school he may find that the school play is, quite literally, a *school* play. It involves the school as a whole. Staff and pupils are not only aware that it is being rehearsed, but are in many cases actively involved in it. The set is being designed under the supervision of the art master and constructed under the supervision of the woodwork master. The physics staff will be complaining about the inadequacies of the lighting equipment, whilst the domestic science mistress will be wondering how she can get the money for all that crossgartering. One or two members of staff may quietly regard the whole activity as a complete waste of time, but at least they will be aware that some activity is taking place. The play will come in for some comment, or even recrimination, at Staff Meetings. The headmaster will make reference to it at Assembly, along with his references to the performance of the rugby 1st XV.

In the poor speech school, the pattern may be quite different. One master, with a particular interest in the theatre, may share his responsibilities with no other staff member. He will not involve the whole of 5B, but only those two or three members of it with a considerable interest in the theatre. In consequence, his play may reach a higher level of theatrical achievement than that of the good speech school, but it is a school play only in the sense that it involves a very select group of school members, and that it takes place in the school hall.

The Debating Society

Public debate requires a high degree of skill in oral communication.

The good speech school will have a society that conducts regular and frequent meetings. Its motions will be given publicity, not only on approved places on notice boards, but in Assembly. It will be attended by considerable numbers of school members. These members will include both pupils and staff. Speeches will by no means be restricted to the platform; they will be made with some vigour and sense of involvement from the floor. The visitor will think to himself: 'these people behave as if they thought this activity important'.

The visitor may find that the debating society in the poor speech school is essentially removed from the activity of the school as a whole. He will think to himself not, 'these people behave as if they thought this activity important', but, 'these people behave as if they ought to think this activity important'.

Other Oral Activities

There may be other oral activities in which both schools engage. Both may conduct internal verse speaking contests. Both may insist that members of the upper school take it in turn to read aloud in Assembly. But an investigation of what lies behind these activities, will show a fundamental difference of approach on the part of the two schools.

Importance

The visitor's final judgment on the two schools will be that the good speech school regards skill in oral communication as important. The poor speech school regards such skill as being no more than a social frill, not in any way fundamental to the education of a fully developed human being.

No speech education can take place unless the head, the staff, and the pupils attach a genuine importance to skill in oral communication. A school may appoint a specialist in speech education to its staff. But unless the work of such a person is seen as a vital contribution to the total education of a human being, such an appointment will be useless.

Opportunities

Speech education requires opportunities for practice. In a good speech school we will find many such opportunities, although not necessarily under the particular heading of speech education. We will find oral work in class in connection with a wide range of subjects. Importance will be attached to oral skill in modern languages. Much of the study of English dramatic literature will be conducted orally. The study of poetry will have a strong oral side. Pupils will feel a certain freedom to express themselves orally in class, whatever subject is being taught. Outside the classroom, pupils will feel that an oral contact with the staff is possible, and actively encouraged.

Outside formal classroom work there will be opportunities to engage in a wide range of oral activities—dramatic activities, debating, speech festivals. Everyone at some stage will be expected to make some oral contribution in Assembly. On those occasions when parents visit the school, pupils will be available to explain to them the school's various activities.

The Staff as Speech Models

It is most important that a child whose speech development concerns us, should be faced regularly by teachers whose speech is worthy of imitation.

We have seen that words are rather insubstantial things for carrying meaning, when they are in conflict with other aspects of the total communicative act. And this justifies, from another point of view, the requirement for a reasonable standard of speech from the teacher. It is not sufficient for him to say, 'I regard speech as an important part of the educational development of the child.' He himself must have speech that backs up this assertion.

How Is the Teacher to Assess His Own Speech?

At the moment very little attention is paid in teacher training to the speech of potential teachers. In consequence, a teacher taking up his first post cannot assume automatically that his speech is a satisfactory model for his pupils, merely because he has been through some process of general professional training. Nor can he get any useful impression of his speech simply by talking to himself and listening to the result. Any good-quality recording-apparatus will show him at once that the difference between the speech that he hears inside his head and the speech that other people hear from him is fundamental.

But there are four things he might do:

i He can listen to recordings of his speech made on apparatus of high fidelity. When we discuss the use of such apparatus in the conduct of speech education, we shall see that it has considerable limitations. But such an approach will give him at least a general idea of his success, or lack of it, on such points as audibility, intelligibility and flexibility.

ii More usefully, he can take the advice of a specialist listener. He must pick such a person with care. It would be useless to pick a person with a deep and emotional prejudice against the type of local pronunciation that the speaker has. In such a case, the comments of the listener would be useless. He must pick someone with specialist knowledge of the subject, so that he can be sure that any comments arise from a rational view of the subject and a clearly defined end-product. He must pick someone who will make comments which are not so much objectively true, as useful.

iii He can assess his speech in terms of its effect on a group of listeners. This assessment is, in the end, the only valid one. Speech that communicates successfully in the classroom is successful speech.

When a teacher speaks to a class, that class will react to him. Suppose the front three rows keep their eyes on him whilst the back row chats quietly. He can tell certain things about his speech from this mixed reaction. The relationship he has created with the front three rows has not extended to the back of the class. The volume he is using is sufficient for most of the class, but not for those sitting farthest from him. If the acoustics of the room are poor, or there is a good deal of outside noise, his articulation may not be sufficiently precise to make his statements entirely intelligible to those on the back row.

Experiment will show him on which of these points he is failing. If he decides to strengthen the relationship, for example, before he speaks, he will look deliberately round the class to see exactly where every child is sitting. He will focus his attention particularly on those children sitting farthest from him. He will remind himself of their names. He may decide to address a remark to one or two of them— 'Smith, are you listening?'—simply to increase his contact with them. As he speaks he will remind himself that it is his job to maintain this contact with every member of the class and through this contact to pass information. If the children on the back row still show little interest in what he is saying, he will need to experiment along other lines.

He can experiment with the volume of sound he is making, and he can experiment with articulation.

Denied specialist advice, this approach of experimenting with different types of voice and speech and testing their effect on a group of listeners, is perhaps the most important open to the teacher for assessing the success of his own speech.

iv   We have mentioned the fact that voice and speech are produced by parts of the human mechanism designed primarily for other purposes. A teacher can make a fourth assessment of his own speech by assessing the amount of strain speaking produces in him. If he finds, at the end of a day's teaching, that his throat is frequently sore, he can be sure he is placing more strain on the vocal mechanism than it is designed to bear.

Speech and the Involvement of all Staff

The responsibility for the development of successful oral communication, cannot be handed over entirely to one member of staff. Even in those schools where there is a staff member with specialist qualifications in the subject, all staff can enhance or hinder his function by their attitude to the subject.

Some subjects, Modern Languages and English, for example, appear to lend themselves particularly well to an oral approach. Others, History and Physics, for example, appear not to. But an oral approach is to some extent possible whatever the subject taught.

C

How to Prevent Speech

Our aim is to encourage the development of fluent oral communication. In this context it might be useful to see how speech can be prevented altogether. We shall then have a negative view of how we might encourage its development.

Most of the factors involved in inhibiting speech will be apparent if we construct a hypothetical staff-meeting. The headmaster has become convinced that some improvement in the speech of the school is necessary:

HEAD: I think we need to conduct a real blitz on speech. We don't want any more of this slipshod chatter that's going on at the moment.

JONES: (*English specialist; high-pitched voice; very precise articulation*) Can you give us some guidance, headmaster?

HEAD: Well, we must make it clear throughout the school that bad speech won't be tolerated. If you hear bad speech in the playground then you must stop it. If two boys are talking at a noticeboard—suppose it's a football notice—you know the kind of thing; 'We 'aven' gorra chance agin them' —well, they must be stopped and made to say it properly. . . .

BROWN: (*Physicist; clear, intelligible speech; strong Cockney accent*) What about the science staff? I don't know anything about speech.

HEAD: Oh, come, Mr Brown. You can tell good speech from bad speech. There's nothing difficult there, surely.

SIMPSON: (*Historian; hoarse voice; loses his voice twice a term*) Is this just out of class, headmaster?

HEAD: Of course not. Wherever you hear bad speech, jump on it firmly.

If the head's request is carried out conscientiously, the result will be the cessation of all speech that is not absolutely essential throughout the school. No child is going to risk being overheard chatting to a friend in the corridor, if there is a chance that his speech will be 'jumped on firmly'.

A school, determined to inhibit the development of speech, might draw up a table of rules like this:

1   The staff must have conflicting views of what kind of speech is successful.

2   Insist on speech that is 'correct'.

3   Comment on pronunciation, particularly in emotionally loaded and vague terms: 'vulgar', 'crude'.

4   Comment on voice quality, particularly in terms of personality: 'effeminate', 'wishy-washy'.

5   All speech comments should be in terms that cannot be made use of by the speaker: 'you sound like Donald Duck', 'you've got a filthy Cockney accent'.

6   Focus a child's attention on his speech in such a way that the whole process is drawn into consciousness. Keep it in his consciousness by frequent and conflicting comments.

7   Insist that a child thinks before he speaks.

8   See that speech conforms to the rules of written language.

9   Make sure that the speech of at least some members of staff fails to reach those standards being required of the child.

10   Roundly condemn the speech of the playground as being 'lazy', 'slipshod', 'crude', 'vulgar' and 'common'. Ignore the fact that it might still be effective as communication in that situation.

11   If a member of staff be appointed with specialist qualifications in the subject, make sure that his efforts in no way impinge on the serious work of the school.

12   Although a certain amount of speech will be inevitable in the Speech Education classes, insist that all other classes be conducted in silence.

Here is an authentic quotation from a class in a Secondary Modern School, conducted by a trainee teacher with a degree in History. It shows in action a number of these points:

> 'There are still some of you who can't work alone. I want no talking at all. I want absolute silence. I want every boy to work by himself. You can't work and talk. The next boy who talks will stay in after school. . . .'

Any reasonable child, hearing statements like these frequently, would draw at least three conclusions from them:

1 Speech means lack of work.
2 Speech means disobedience.
3 Speech means punishment.

This particular student teacher was probably doing no more than regurgitating statements that he himself had heard during his own school life But it is significant that his own speech did not reach those standards required for successful teaching.

3
The Speech Specialist

Some few schools have on their staffs, teachers with specialist qualifications in speech. There is already a tendency to employ more of such people in schools. Such teachers, if they are to have any marked effect on oral studies, will need to be given the same freedom to operate throughout the school as are other members of staff with more traditional subjects. But we cannot say what the position of such a person should be in a school unless we know something about the training he has undergone and the sort of problems of oral communication he is able to deal with.

In society at the moment, the only person who stands or falls absolutely on his ability to communicate orally, is the actor. The clergyman, the teacher and the lawyer may all be less than competent in oral communication, but they will not be dismissed on this count alone. This is not true of the actor. An actor who is unskilled in oral communication will never be employed. It is the absolute essential of his profession. It is understandable, therefore, that the serious study of speech as communication is still restricted to a handful of theatre schools. Our specialist, if his qualifications in speech are considerable, will inevitably be a product of one of these schools. This fact is significant, if we are to understand his approach. If he is young, he may appear to us to spend rather a lot of time in dramatic activities. The reason is obvious; the only continuous tradition of oral studies lies in the theatre and his own training in such studies has inevitably been conducted in relation to the needs of the theatre. But the head and staff of a school can be expected to show an interest in what he is trying to do; such an interest will encourage him to extend his view of the subject so that it includes the whole field of speech situations.

His specialist training might have taken one, two or three years. It will have included such subjects as:

1 *Anatomy and Physiology as applied to Speech*

He will have a close knowledge of the construction and function of the larynx. He will have a knowledge of the anatomy and physiology of the head and neck, and a particular knowledge of those parts which directly affect speech and hearing. He will have a close knowledge of the anatomy and physiology of the chest as related to breathing. He will have a general knowledge of anatomy and physiology as applied to movement.

2 *Physics of Sound*

He will have some knowledge of the way sound is produced and perceived. He will know the effect of passing a fundamental note into a hollow space. He will know something of the physics of resonators.

3 *Psychology as applied to Speech and Movement*

He will have made a general study of elementary psychology, and a more particular study of those aspects directly concerned with voice, speech and movement. He will have, as a result of this study, an insight into those psychological processes which inform speech and movement. He will know that speech education involves not only changes in the external aspects of speech, but alterations in those psychological processes that lie behind speech.

4 *Theory of Voice and Speech Education*

He will have had a thorough grounding in the theory of Voice and Speech Education. He will know what education can do and what it cannot do in developing voice and speech. He will know how this body of theoretical knowledge can be applied in practice. He will know quite clearly what successful speech is in a given situation. He will know the point at which unsuccessful speech becomes subnormal speech.

5 *Phonetics*

He will have made a study of general phonetic theory, and its application to the sounds of spoken English. He will have some knowledge of the phonetics of two or three European languages. It is unlikely that he will make any attempt to teach phonetics as a subject, since this is not his main concern. But he will use his phonetic knowledge as a tool in the diagnosis of certain speech problems, and in the changing of certain articulatory habits. For example, if he comes across a child who substitutes something like a 'w' for the 'r' in 'red', 'rabbit', 'very', he will know how this child produces this substitution, what he needs to do to produce the more usual sound, and how the more usual sound may be taught and finally incorporated in the child's speech.

6 *English Poetry and Prose*

He will have made a considerable study of English literature. This study will have been conducted to a large extent in oral terms. He will have, in consequence, a view of literature that places as much stress upon its emotional and intuitive aspects as upon its intellectual, and pays considerable attention to such factors as rhythm and form. He will favour the reading aloud of poetry as a method of study, rather than the more orthodox and traditional approach of silent reading followed by stress upon the intellectual content.

7 *Practical studies*

Side by side with his more theoretical studies, he will have done a lot of practical work. He will have done continuous work on his own speech processes over a considerable period of time, and this will have done three things: it will have developed his own speech skills and those processes that inform them; it will have given him a very clear view of his own speech; it will have given him an insight into what is involved in the process of speech education.

He will have an ability, through a great deal of practice, to speak verse and prose aloud to other people, in such a way as to convey to them the total intention of the writer.

He will have done a good deal of practical work designed to develop his own skill in general movement.

8   Dramatic studies

He will have made a study in detail of the History of Drama, the Development of the Theatre and the Nature of Acting. He will have had considerable practical experience in theatre studies.

9   Professional training

He will have been through a teacher-training programme that will have shown him the methods by which he can apply his knowledge for educational purposes.

What can we expect such a person to do if he is appointed to the staff of a school as a speech educationist? We can expect him to be responsible for speech education throughout the school, for the planning of speech programmes and for teaching. We can expect him to exert some general influence on school activities that will bring oral activities more into focus in all classes. We can expect him to engage in such out-of-school activities as the school play, the debating society and the speech festival.

We can expect him to help individual children with particular problems of speech which he considers to be within his province. We can expect him to advise on those children whose speech is so defective that they need the attention of a speech therapist.

We can expect him to help with such established subjects as English, by reinforcing the work of the English staff. We can expect him to help with class dramatic activities.

We can expect his comments in staff meetings on those aspects of school life which he thinks are enhancing or retarding the speech development of the children.

We can expect him to wish to enter a selected number of children for the tests in Spoken English conducted by the C.S.E. and G.C.E. examining bodies, with a view to checking his success against that of other schools in the country.

Admitted as a responsible and necessary member of the school community, he can transform the speech of the children as a tool for communication. Relegated to the position of a specialist whose work has little bearing on the business of preparing children for G.C.E. or C.S.E., he will influence only those children whose oral skill is already considerable.

4

Comments on Speech

At present, few schools employ a specialist teacher in Speech Education. This position is likely to continue for some years. The number of such teachers is very small, and there appear to be no plans for increasing it. The onus for developing the speech processes of the child, will inevitably fall on the non-specialist.

Given opportunities to speak in situations removed from the playground, the child will inevitably show some speech development, on a purely trial-and-error basis. But education requires more than this. It requires some external direction, some comment that will guide this development in a coherent way. We are faced, then, with the question: What speech comment will be of value to the child?

Listener-Reception, not Speaker-Performance

There are two distinct views from which we can comment. We can comment in terms of what effect a speaker has upon us as a listener, or we can comment in terms of what the speaker is doing. For example, if a speaker is not loud enough we can say one of two things. We can say, 'I cannot hear you', or 'You are not loud enough'. The first comment implies an involvement on our part in the communication situation. Here is a speaker, and here we are as listeners. The comment is seen by the speaker as a legitimate clue from a listener which indicates a failure on his part to do what he intended to do. The second comment is made from a different standpoint. It is not the comment of a listener from within the situation, but of an observer standing outside the situation. As such, the speaker does not immediately see its relevance, nor indeed what exactly to do to correct the fault. It was not his intention to communicate with an observer outside the situation, but with a listener actively involved in it. 'Who is this person,' he appears to think, 'making comments on my speech? I was trying to pass information to a listener, not to someone outside.'

The first principle, then, of speech comment, is this:

i   Comment must be made from the point of view of the listener.

Science and Magic

An understanding of the scientific principles behind a piece of apparatus is in many cases sufficient for the user to be able to operate it successfully. A monkey can twiddle the taps of a gas cooker, but if he is not asphyxiated he will be fortunate. If he succeeds in boiling himself an egg, it will be a miracle. Yet a housewife of average competence can cook dinner on the same apparatus day after day. She can do so because she knows what the apparatus is designed to do, and how it does it. A housewife unfamiliar with the apparatus can be taught to use it very quickly, by having the scientific principles explained to her.

Unfortunately—and it is unfortunate—this approach has a very limited use in speech work. A specific example will make the point clearer: suppose we meet a child with a husky voice and for one reason or another we wish to change this. Investigation might show that the cause is the incomplete closure of the vocal cords. The solution will be a greater degree of contraction of certain muscles of the larynx, in particular the crico-arytenoids and the inter-arytenoids. We can imagine the situation:

TEACHER: All you need to do, John, is contract the crico-arytenoids and the inter-arytenoids.

JOHN: Thank you sir. . . . How?

TEACHER: Well. . . .

Even assuming a considerable knowledge of the anatomy of

the larynx on John's part, the information he has been given will not change his huskiness one wit. As he says, he does not know how to get conscious control over the movement of the muscles of the larynx. Nor does anyone else, not in this direct way. His complaint is not that the information is inaccurate, but that it is useless.

What are we to say to John, then? We might say to him that voice has nothing to do with the vocal cords. We might tell him that it is made on the lips or even in front of the lips. We might go still further and tell him that voice is made in the listener's ear and has very little to do with the speaker. This is manifestly untrue, if we view it as a description of what is happening. Yet this 'image' of its being made in the listener's ear will produce the vocal change that we are after, in a way that a scientifically accurate description of what is happening never will.

We are faced, then, with an apparent and quite fundamental conflict between what is scientifically accurate and what will produce the results that we are after. At this point we must be quite clear of our intention. If it is to give a scientifically acceptable description of what is happening in the production of a given voice, then we should not expect any change in that voice as a result of that description. But if it is to change and develop that voice, then we must be prepared to employ comment that may appear little short of magic.

How Do We Know what Comments to Make?

This imagery has its own logic. We cannot make any sort of wild comment, simply because it differs from the description of what is happening. We must use that imagery that can be interpreted as meaningful by the speaker, and can be put to profitable use by him. We can build up by experience an appreciation of the kind of imagery that is useful and the kind that is useless. For example, experience will tell us that though it is physiologically inaccurate to say either, 'Your voice should be made in front of your face' or 'Your voice should be made at the back of your throat', one is useful whilst the other is
68

useless. One produces the result we are after; the other produces a quite different result.

Future research might show that a particular image is not universally applicable; but for the moment we cannot go further than ask ourselves of any image that we propose to use, 'What effect would such a comment have on me? How would I interpret it?'

Two further principles of comment follow from this:

ii   Comment should be usable by the person to whom it is made.

iii   Since speech functions most satisfactorily when it is not a conscious process, comment should focus the speaker's attention away from himself and towards the listener.

'Your voice is made in front of your face' is a useful comment from this third point of view. It begins to focus a speaker's attention away from himself and towards the object of his communication. 'Your voice is made in the back of your throat' is not a useful comment; if focuses the speaker's attention on himself rather than on the object of the communication.

Personality Comments

Some comments that we make about a person's speech will not be interpreted by him in speech terms at all, but in terms of the personality behind his speech. If we tell him that his speech is vulgar, he will not see this as a comment on his speech, but upon himself. 'My speech is essentially myself,' he appears to be saying. 'If it is vulgar, then I am vulgar.' Such a comment is aimed too deeply, since even if the comment does not arouse in him an attitude of acute resentment, he does not know what he can do to change his offending personality. The comment, even if it were seen by the speaker as referring to nothing more fundamental than his outward speech, is useless; it tells him what the listener sees to be wrong, without giving him the slightest indication of what he might do to put it right.

Speech is, of course, intimately associated with the personality of the person using it. But comment about this personality is rarely useful. We might lay down a fourth principle concerning the comments that we should make to a speaker, like this:

iv   Such comments should be made in such a way that they will be interpreted by the speaker as speech comments, rather than comments directed at the personality behind the speech.

Comments that might be misinterpreted

We have seen that some comments which are highly useful to a speaker, may be made in terms of imagery rather than in terms of scientifically acceptable description. It is essential that when we make a comment, both we and the speaker know whether the comment is one of imagery or description.

Some voices are very widely described as being 'high-pitched', for example. If the speaker knows a little about the mechanism of voice and speech, and he sees the comment as a description of what he is doing, he will begin work directly on the pitch of his voice. If, on the other hand, he sees the comment as an image used by the listener to convey to him the impression his voice gives the listener, he will aim at producing a voice that will give the listener an impression of being 'lower-pitched' or even 'low-pitched'. In the first case he will work on the length and tension of his vocal cords; in the second case he will work on the resonating system. Both approaches will produce quite different results.

As a fifth principle of comment, then, we can say:

v   The person commenting on voice and speech should be quite clear whether his comments are in terms of description or imagery. They should be given in terms that will be correctly interpreted by the speaker.

Comments by the rest of the class

Our comments as teachers on the voice and speech of a particular child, should be very valuable to him. But so should the comments of others to whom he is speaking. In classwork, these comments will be made by his contemporaries. Some comments will be useful; many will be useless:

'He's too quick.'
'I couldn't hear him.'
'He sounded like an elephant talking through its trunk.'
'There's something wrong with his mouth.'
'He was reading to himself.'
'He sounds sissy.'
'I couldn't understand him.'

'He's too quick', 'I couldn't hear him', 'He was reading to himself' and 'I couldn't understand him', are comments that the speaker might conceivably find of use. But what is he to make of 'He sounds like an elephant talking through its trunk'? 'There's something wrong with his mouth' suggests all kinds of alarming deformities, and 'He sounds sissy' strikes so deeply into his view of himself that it could well stop him talking in front of others forever. But if we are clear what the next step in his speech development should be and what comments will be of use to him in taking this next step, we can guide the rest of the class in such a way as to produce those comments.

Suppose we decide that what he needs above everything at the moment is to be encouraged to make more noise. We might get the useful comments that we need from the class, in this way:

TEACHER: Now what about the people on the front row; could you hear him?
FRONT ROW: Yes.
TEACHER: Good. Well, that's an improvement, John. Was he too loud for you?
FRONT ROW: No.
TEACHER: Good. Well, as far as the front row's concerned, John, you've been successful. Now hands up those people in the middle rows who had a little difficulty in hearing him.
  Some hands go up.
TEACHER: Your hand isn't up, William. Could you hear him all right?

71

WILLIAM: Yes, I could hear him.

TEACHER: Well, you're reaching some people in the middle rows now. Look at the people with their hands up. They're the ones you want to concentrate on. Try it again. The rest of you, keep your hands up until you can hear him all right, then put them down. Now John; make them all put their hands down. . . .

Speech Before Speech Education

In making comments on speech we must bear in mind that we cannot develop speech unless we have some speech to develop. Our first comments, then, should be aimed at producing fluent and connected speech. Such speech may be highly unsatisfactory from many points of view, but at this stage this is irrelevant. No comments should be made that inhibit speech, since without speech we have nothing to educate. Only when we have easy, fluent speech, should we begin the process of trying to guide it along paths that will make it more successful.

Normal and Non-Normal Speech

We cannot create speech. We can only develop it if it already exists. Speech Education is essentially the process of developing normal speech in such a way that it will be more successful for those purposes for which it is already being used, and successful for those more complex purposes of which the child has at the moment no experience. Speech Education is not concerned with changing non-normal speech into that which is normal. That is the function of the Speech Therapist.

Before we begin any Speech Education process, then, we need to be quite clear that the speech that is available for us to develop is normal speech. A child who has speech which makes it difficult for him to buy sweets in a shop or make himself understood easily by his colleagues, has speech which is not normal for his age. The severe stammerer can be said to have non-normal speech, because his difficulty interferes seriously with his attempts to use speech for communication purposes. The child who cannot make a large number of the sounds of spoken English can be said to have non-normal speech, because his speech makes communication very difficult if not impossible. Such children should be referred, through the School Medical Officer, to a Speech Therapist.

But the communication test is not entirely satisfactory. It is possible to have a markedly husky voice and still be able to communicate. Yet that huskiness might be the result of nodal growths on the vocal cords. Such growths need the attention of a laryngologist and a Speech Therapist. What we need to do in such cases, is build a concept of normal voice and speech by listening consciously to children's talk. Any child whose speech falls clearly outside this concept, should be referred to a Speech Therapist.

Part Three

Speech in Class

Introduction

To produce the school-leaver who can communicate with ease in a wide range of differing situations, requires some special attention to speech. This part of the book is concerned with the ways in which this special attention may be given by a teacher without specialist qualifications in the subject.

What should be our approach?

There are two possible approaches. The first deals in an analytical way with the various aspects of speech, volume, articulation, pitch, and then reunites them into a whole. The second deals throughout with speech as a total psychophysical process.

The Analytical Approach

The analytical approach is direct. It approaches articulation in terms of exercises designed to increase the speed and accuracy of movements of tongue, jaw, lips and soft-palate. It approaches volume in terms of breathing exercises to increase capacity and to increase the degree of control over the outgoing breath. For example:

1 Shoot the tongue in and out as far and as hard as possible until it is tired. It will then fall naturally into its right position in the mouth.
2 Practise curling the tip and sides of tongue.

J. G. MARASH, *Effective Speaking*, Harrap, 1947.

77

And for breathing:

POSITIONS. Stand easily erect. Feet apart. Head inclined slightly forward. Tips of fingers touching, as in Position 1.

Breathe in, while raising the arms through Position 2 to Position 3. Notice that, with the eyes following the hands, the chin will tilt upwards, allowing the head to swing slightly backwards. In all movements the hand must *follow* the arm.

Breathe out, while lowering the arms slowly through Position 4 back to the first position.

MRS. A. M. HENDERSON, *Good Speaking*, Pan, 1956.

Inevitably, the analytical approach draws into consciousness the physical attributes of speech. The approach requires considerable knowledge of the anatomy and physiology of the mechanism on which speech is dependent. It requires, too, sufficient psychological knowledge to synthesize the new habits and let them return to unconsciousness. If the new habits remain in consciousness, the speaker is in the same position as the unhappy centipede:

The centipede was happy quite
Until the toad, in fun,
Said, 'Pray, which leg comes after which?'
Which worked him up to such a pitch
He lay distracted in a ditch
Considering how to run.

The analytical and direct approach is essential with some children, but it is an approach that is best left to the specialist.

The Whole-Speech Approach

The alternative to the analytical approach, is one which aims to develop the child's speech as a whole. It is an indirect approach in the sense that it focuses the child's attention away from his speech apparatus by involving him completely in some activity that has a significance in itself. It is an approach based on the very sound view that the whole communication process functions best when it is unconscious.

78

The indirect approach, the approach that regards the act of speech communication as an indivisible whole, lends itself admirably to use in the classroom by the teacher without specialist training in the subject. For this reason it is the approach on which all the work suggested in this part of the book is based.

I

An Approach Through Drama

The theatre is worthy of study in its own right, but this is not our concern here. We are concerned with dramatic activity as a method, not as an end. The dramatic approach to speech work is particularly useful since it allows us imaginatively to recreate those real-life situations in which satisfactory playground speech has already developed, and then develop such situations in ways that place more and more demands on speech.

Initially we want a dramatic method that will produce some continuous, sensible speech, in keeping with the demands of a particular situation. We need, ideally, a room that is large and unfurnished. The school hall or gymnasium is usually most successful, but a large classroom can be quite satisfactory if the desks can be moved sufficiently to leave a working space in which the class has some freedom of movement. Since the class is going to make a noise—that being our sole aim—we should have a room that will allow the noise to be made without the restriction of feeling that other classes are being disturbed.

Mime

No mention is made of speech. Any speech that arises should be regarded as incidental to the central activity. Everyone is involved. There is no 'audience factor' which the children engaged in the activity sense as a critical element judging the success of what they are doing.

The children work initially as individuals, not as a group.

80

In front of each of them is a large, imaginary rock on the floor. They are to bend down and, using their hands, discover its exact size, shape and texture. Then they are to lift it. How they lift it will depend on its weight, shape, size and texture. No speech will be required at this stage. Nothing in the situation demands it. It is possible to inspect a rock, pick it up and return it to its place, without reference to spoken language.

Speech will almost certainly appear if individual activity ceases and even the smallest groups are formed. The children are put into pairs and told to lift between them a heavy object on the floor. To lift such an object it must be defined. Its length and breadth and texture must be known. So must its weight. For two children to agree on these factors, speech is necessary.

'What does he want us to lift?'

'This thing.'

'What is it?'

'Well—it's a log.'

'Or a plank.'

'That's easier—a plank.'

'And it's about this long, and about this wide.'

'Get your end—now. . . .'

This is connected speech which has arisen from the needs of a particular situation. All the elements of successful speech are present. To extend the speech, the situation can be extended.

Instead of concentrating on the object to be lifted, concentration can be shifted to the endproduct. If we build a pyramid, heavy objects will need to be moved by the class. The aim, however, is no longer the moving of such objects, but the actual building. Groups will be of five or six. In order to work successfully, more detailed speech will be necessary.

'It's a great slab of stone.'

'It's going to be heavy.'

'It's not a slab. It's been cut. It'll be square.'

'Rectangular.'

'How big is it?'

'Up to here. And about—this long.'

'We can't shift that.'

'No, it's about this high, and that wide and as long as—this.'

'That's better.'

'Let's push it.'

They lean on one end of it and decide it won't move.

'It's too heavy.'

'Hm!'

'Can't we lift it?'

'If we can't push it, of course we can't lift it.'

'What about rolling it?'

'On what?'

'Some rollers.'

'We haven't got any rollers.'

'We'll cut down some trees.'

'What with?'

'We could pull it with ropes. . . .'

At least we are producing fluent speech, even though so far the pyramid remains unbuilt. The situation can be made still more complex. This is not *any* pyramid they are building; it is an *Egyptian* pyramid to receive the body of a king. Now there are many other factors to be considered. They are slaves operating under the whip in a temperature of 100° Fahrenheit. How long have they been working today already? What do they feel about their condition? How much longer are they prepared to put up with it? Introduce two slavedrivers, anxious at all costs to increase production, and the situation will become explosive. Certainly it will produce an abundance of connected speech arising from the needs of a particular situation.

Crowd Work

Where the mime approach ends and the more fully dramatic begins, is difficult to say. Crowd Work is certainly a legitimate form of drama. It is improvised and unscripted. Speech is essential to it. It involves the whole class. No one sits on the fringes of the activity watching it.

We might begin with a fairground. We shall need some chairs, placed together in pairs or threes, to represent stalls.

If we are in the gymnasium we can use benches, or the box, or even the buck. These should not be placed too far apart since the activity needs a certain physical concentration. We shall require stallholders, two to each stall. Four or five pairs should be sufficient. Initially, we should select the more voluble members of the class to help the quick development of the activity. The stallholders will decide what kind of stall they are running—a rifle range, a rolling penny stand, a coconut shy. Bingo is too static an activity to be very helpful here. As the stallholders begin to cry out their various entertainments, the rest of the class walks into the fairground. They are instructed simply to take advantage of the various activities offered by the stallholders.

Unless the class is experienced in this kind of work, it is unlikely that anything very useful will develop from the first few minutes. John and Gerald will continue to behave as John and Gerald. John is unlikely to say very much; Gerald is likely to be bossy in a disrupting way. When we stop the scene for the first time, it is unlikely that the class will have done much more than caught on to what is expected of them. The sort of useful comments we might make are those designed to produce more general freedom, and in particular more freedom of speech.

We might single out a particular small group round one of the stalls for a word of praise for its vulgar or its wholehearted involvement in throwing balls at imaginary coconuts. We might tell John that the way he simply stood quietly to one side, was impressive. We shall know, of course, that he did this because he felt entirely lost in being asked to immerse himself in a fairground in the middle of the school gymnasium. But he will interpret it as being an encouragement that allows him to be a little more adventurous.

We shall find, as the activity continues, that what we had thought would be our major difficulty—getting the class to produce ideas, and therefore speech—is in fact no difficulty at all. The real difficulty is in controlling the development of such ideas. Without any prompting from us we might find this development round the coconut shy:

GERALD: (*throwing a ball venomously past the stallholder*) There! What'd I tell you!

STALLHOLDER: Well?

GERALD: I want me prize.

STALLHOLDER: What prize?

GERALD: For knocking off a coconut.

STALLHOLDER: You never knocked one off.

GERALD: What's that then, that on the floor?

STALLHOLDER: That was there before.

GERALD: No, it wasn't.

STALLHOLDER: Yes, it was.

GERALD: I knocked it off.

STALLHOLDER: No, you didn't.

WILKINS: I saw him.

STALLHOLDER: You couldn't have.

GERALD: I'll bust up your stall!

POLICEMAN: 'Ere, 'ere, 'ere. What's all this then?

We may not be aesthetically or grammatically too happy with the speech itself. But we cannot deny that it is fluent and vigorous speech which, within this situation, does its job creditably. At least we have heard something which could be developed educationally. We may not know what prompted Briggs to transform himself into a policeman at that precise moment. But the situation certainly demanded the intervention of some authority, and Briggs appreciated this demand. Briggs went further. He ceased to be Briggs. He gave a very crude and comic picture of a policeman, but it was a picture of a policeman and not simply Briggs being funny.

We should remind ourselves at this point, that what we are principally concerned with is the development of speech. If we were concerned with drama as drama here, we should be tempted to develop this scene. What happens after the policeman's intervention? Does Gerald go quietly away? Is he taken off by the policeman? Does he try to damage the stall? Has he friends with him? But we must balance such a development against the special needs of the class as a whole. Gerald is certainly prepared to talk already, whereas John has not so far said a word.

Fortunately, whilst Gerald's outburst was in progress, John was engaged in a microscopic activity. He was just raising the tips of his fingers towards the pocket of the boy next to him. He seemed to be quite unaware of the main scene at the coconut shy, and yet what he was doing had some significance within the total situation. In view of the need to get some connected speech from John in a situation that makes him feel a little out of his depth, it is this tiny movement of his that we will wish to develop.

'Very good, Gerald,' we might say. 'But whilst everyone's watching your quarrel, nobody's noticed the pickpocket down here quietly robbing people. This time, John, I'd like you to be caught with your hand actually in that boy's pocket. . . .'

Gerald's scene will establish the policeman, the policeman will be bound to question John and John will have to give some explanation in speech terms.

The scene can be made more complex still, if we think it useful in provoking more vocal reaction, by changing the weather conditions or the time of day. We might concentrate on the speech of the stallholders by beginning the scene early in the morning before the fairground is open to the public. Stalls would have to be erected and then set out. For the success of such an activity, speech would be essential.

The Development of Speech

Once speech has begun to appear with some ease and fluency, it can be developed. The possibilities of the dramatic approach for such development, are almost limitless. Within the dramatic framework, a very wide variety of differing situations can be engineered, each situation making different demands on the speech of those involved.

Volume

We can experiment with volume in one of two ways:

i By increasing the physical size of the situation in which the dramatic activity is taking place.

   ii By creating a situation in which considerable volume is necessary.

In the case of the fairground, we can increase the distance between one group and the next simply by pushing the stalls further apart. Any stallholder who wishes to communicate with a friend at another stall will have to use more volume. This he will do automatically if he sees that the increased distance requires it. In most cases there will be little need for us to comment on his efforts; he will see at once whether he has succeeded or not in doing what he intended, by the reaction, or lack of it, of the friend to whom he was calling.

Considerable volume will be necessary if we create a situation that is noisy and excited, and then ask someone to speak above the noise. Suppose that instead of using the fairground scene, we begin in the marketplace. Much the same developments will take place. We shall have stallholders and customers. From somewhere we shall need a policeman. When it is clear to us that everyone is involved in buying or selling, or simply arguing, we can change the direction of the activity like this:

TEACHER: All right. . . . One thing I'm not clear about: where is this marketplace?

BOY 1: It's in a small town.

TEACHER: Yes, but what country?

BOY 2: England, sir.

TEACHER: What would be the difference if it were in South America?

BOY 1: Sir, it would be hotter.

GIRL 1: It would be noisier.

TEACHER: (*We know from past experience that Girl 1 would be noisy, even if we set the scene in a church at Evensong. But her statement fits in so exactly without intention, that we get her to develop it.*) Noisier—why?

GIRL 1: Well, they're hotblooded. That makes them noisy.

TEACHER: (*We suspect that she sees herself as 'hotblooded' and therefore noisy.*) Hotblooded? What do you mean by hotblooded?

GIRL 1: Well—excitable.

TEACHER: So it would be hotter. The people would be excitable and this would make them speak more loudly—is that right?

BOY 2: Yes sir.

So we have a situation that will encourage more noise. Everyone will experiment, without doing so consciously, with increased volume. But who can benefit particularly from the situation? Clearly, only someone with the authority to impose silence upon the entire group. He must produce considerable volume if he is to be heard, but once he is heard and recognized his authority will be sufficient to silence everyone quite quickly. We cannot use our policeman for such a purpose. His authority is not such that he can command absolute silence from a noisy crowd in a marketplace. But in certain circumstances we might use an army officer, particularly if he were supported by two or three armed men. Suppose that this market scene takes place in a small South American town on the brink of revolution. Amongst the crowd are two or three revolutionaries, perhaps actively preaching revolution. At the height of the activity an army officer runs in supported by three armed men, and commands silence. He has the authority of arms to impose absolute silence on the entire gathering. What will such a situation do from a speech viewpoint? It will allow everyone to make a good deal of noise; to experiment in an indirect way with volume. It will allow four people, the officer and his three men, to make as much noise as they wish. It will define for everyone the difference between considerable volume and complete silence and it will do so in a way that does not focus conscious attention on the process. The aim of the exercise appears to be dramatic; the result is a deeper realization of the amount of noise a particular situation demands and of the volume each person is able to produce. Such a situation might be quite new for many children; those from nonvocal homes will be experiencing for the first time the demands of a highly vocal and very noisy situation. They will appreciate, too, what they must personally do to cope with it.

Articulation

It is possible through the dramatic approach to give opportunities for the practice of a more precise kind of articulation. There are two main lines of approach:

i Through changing the situation in such a way that it demands a greater articulatory precision if a speaker is to cope with it.

ii Through the concentration on the kind of character who is generally represented as speaking precisely.

We might change the situation like this: Suppose the scene is a prison camp. Prisoners stand about the compound. Guards patrol within earshot but out of sight. A small group of prisoners, four or five at the most, are planning an escape. The situation is such that they cannot communicate with one another in anything more than a whisper. Everything they say must be immediately understood by the others, since there may be no opportunity for repetition. We shall find that the restrictions of such a situation produce an increase in articulatory precision, since only in that way can the restrictions be overcome. It is essential, of course, that the guards, though within easy earshot, are out of sight. If they can see the prisoners, then those plotting escape will tend to reduce rather than increase articulatory movement, since such movement is quite obvious to anyone who can see the speaker.

We can make the situation a little more difficult by having a single guard sitting in the middle of the compound, dozing into sleep. The prisoners will feel even more acutely the need to keep noise to a minimum. But since the guard can be seen by them to be asleep, they will feel still freer to increase articulatory movement.

Suppose the guard wakes up. He realizes that something has been going on, though he is not sure what. He sees the tight group of prisoners, perhaps looking a little sheepish, and separates them. He goes back to his seat and again falls asleep. How are they to communicate now? They cannot move together again without being heard. They cannot speak, even in whispers, because the volume required to bridge the distance that separates them will be more than enough to wake the guard. But if they move their articulatory organs with sufficient precision, it is possible for them to be understood, by a process of lip-reading. If we wished to demonstrate to the class that human communication involves a good deal more than words, or even sound, we could develop the situation further. With the seated guard very lightly asleep, we could pick three children in different parts of the compound and ask them to plan and execute an escape. If we watch them we shall see that they employ lip-reading to some extent, but they will also employ all the visual aspects of communication that are open to them. Assuming their escape plan to be sound, its success will be entirely dependent on their ability to communicate visually.

At one time an advertisement appeared regularly on television, based on the fact that the noise in a cotton mill was so great that communication in terms of sound was impossible. Speech communication was conducted in terms of lip-reading. To be effective, this could only take place if the articulatory movements of the speaker were extremely precise. We might use such a fact dramatically. Suppose we go back to our South American marketplace. We have all the ingredients we need here. There is considerable noise, because that is one of the things we have been working for. We have a gathering on the brink of revolution. We have a revolutionary actively stirring up trouble amongst groups of citizens. On the edge of the crowd is a sympathizer who sees the approaching army officer. He cannot call out above the noise of the crowd, because he will draw the officer's attention to him. Nor, for the same reason, can he gesticulate wildly. He can do no more than catch the revolutionary's eye and mouth a warning to him. Such a warning must be precise since, if it is not understood immediately, it will fail in its purpose.

We can give a child experience in using more precise articulatory movements, by commenting on the character he has created. John has created a pickpocket of indiscriminate character. We have reached the point at which John's pickpocket is caught and questioned by the policeman:

D

POLICEMAN: Now then; you took that wallet out of his pocket, didn't you?

JOHN: No, sir.

POLICEMAN: Then what's it doing in your hand?

JOHN: I found it. It was lying on the ground and I picked it up.

POLICEMAN: And I suppose you were just going to hand it back to him?

JOHN: No.

POLICEMAN: Oh!

JOHN: I didn't know it was his. . . .

At this point we can interrupt:

TEACHER: I'm not quite clear what sort of a person this pickpocket is, John. Can you tell me something about him?

JOHN: Well . . . he's old. (*Naturally, he hasn't thought about this aspect of what he was doing. He will need to have some possibilities put before him.*)

TEACHER: Has he picked pockets before?

JOHN: Well . . . no.

TEACHER: Why did he do it then?

JOHN: He had no money.

TEACHER: Before that he'd had plenty of money—is that what you mean?

JOHN: Yes—he used to be a bank manager.

TEACHER: Did he? And how old is he, did you say?

JOHN: He's about fifty.

TEACHER: All right. Let's go back to where you are caught. Now remember this time that you're a man of fifty who used to be a bank manager.

It will be surprising if, in the light of this discussion, John does not make some adjustment to his speech. He will probably go a little more slowly and articulate a little more carefully. If we wish to push him further, we can do so by further comment on the needs of the character:

TEACHER: You know, I think he should be older than fifty, John. Can you make him very old? Make him eighty, will you?

Or, if we find it necessary, we can make the point that we are anxious to develop even more specific:

TEACHER: If he's eighty, how will this affect his behaviour?
JOHN: He'll be slower.
TEACHER: He'll be slower, yes. And what about his speech—will that be affected?
JOHN: That will be slower as well.
TEACHER: Yes of course—slower and more careful, don't you think? Because he's old he walks more carefully so as not to fall, and he speaks more carefully so that his tongue doesn't trip over itself.

Language Style and Pronunciation

This approach to speech through the kind of person who is speaking can be useful in giving experience of other kinds of language and other types of pronunciation than those that the child habitually uses. An aging bank manager will employ a language style and a pronunciation that are different from those that John uses. John, in the character of a bank manager, is free to experiment with these factors in a way that he is not when he is simply himself. The experience resulting from such experiment is something on which he can draw in real-life situations. Experiment has shown him that language that he thought of as impossible for him to use, is not only possible but in certain circumstances very effective.

Flexibility

Ideally, the mechanism of speech should be capable of communicating whatever the speaker wishes to communicate. If the speaker is furious, and he wishes to communicate this fury, his vocal mechanism should be sufficiently flexible to make those sounds that will be understood by a listener as indicative of fury. The dramatic approach allows us opportunities to engineer situations in which these two things can be developed:

i The generation of strong feelings.
ii Their communication in terms of voice and speech.

If we go back to the South American market scene, we shall see how it can be directed for this purpose. Here we have a scene in which feelings are already running high. Revolution is in the air. Power is being held by force of arms. At the pinnacle of power sits a military dictator. Suppose we were to remove this dictator; what would be the outcome? We can try it and see. We should pick two or three children who have not been very vocal, and remove them from the crowd. They are to assassinate the dictator and then announce the fact to the rest of the crowd in the marketplace. The scene will now have six stages:

i The market scene itself, with people buying from the open stalls.

ii The activity of the two or three revolutionaries, trying to fan smouldering discontent into open revolt.

iii The armed men and the officer imposing silence on the scene.

iv The sound, somewhere in the distance, of the assassins' shots.

v The entry of the assassins with the news of the end of the dictatorship.

vi The reaction to the news.

What speech demands does such a situation make on the assassins? Their success should leave them in a turmoil of triumph and excitement. But when they enter the marketplace their friends and relations are being menaced by the guns of four soldiers. The revolution cannot be regarded as successful until those soldiers have been removed. And they can only be removed if the assassins' triumph and excitement are communicated with sufficient force to give the crowd the courage to turn on the soldiers and disarm them. We shall get a clear idea of how successful the communication of the assassins has been, if we do not tell either the crowd or the soldiers that an assassination has been planned. If the assassins are successful, we shall get the reaction we are after without having to brief anyone but the assassins themselves.

If we wish to do more work on this aspect of the speech of

those playing the assassins, we can do so by working on their scene in isolation. We can seat the dictator at his desk in the middle of the room. We can set a guard on his door. We can have the crowd at one end of the room. We can allow the assassins quite a lot of time in approaching the guard and overpowering him, before bursting into the room and shooting the dictator. This will build up the feeling of excitement and apprehension in them and add to their final sense of triumph. The impetus to communicate effectively to the crowd, will in consequence be heightened.

The few words that the assassins cry to the crowd, will hardly be enough to give them the experience that we are after; the experience of disciplining and communicating strong feelings. The situation can be prolonged if the crowd asks them certain obvious questions: What do we do now? What are we to do with the soldiers? What are we to do with the dictator's staff? Who's going to lead us now? What kind of a government shall we have? The conclusion of the scene will be dependent on the replies to questions like this, but a reasonable conclusion would be the exit of the assassins to the government building, followed by the exultant crowd.

The Printed Play

The approach through dramatic crowd work requires no text from which to work. This has considerable advantages. The development of the scene is governed entirely by what we see to be the speech needs of the children. In the printed text the development is confined to the dramatist's requirements. If we are working from the text of *Romeo and Juliet*, then Juliet must die. That conclusion is predetermined. She cannot live simply because we think it would be beneficial to the speech of the child playing her part, for her to do so. The approach through crowd work allows a child to create out of his own experience and imagination any character that he wishes. If we work from the printed text, the child is inevitably restricted to the characters that the dramatist has provided.

But there may be two reasons why we think it necessary to begin from the printed text:

i We are working with older children, already experienced in considering drama as printed text. Such children might feel themselves too sophisticated to relinquish the text at first.
ii We are working within the tight framework of an examination syllabus which requires us to pay close attention to a set play.

If, whilst acknowledging these limitations, we still wish to help in the development of speech, we shall find that it is not impossible to approach the text through crowd work. Suppose for example, that the text that we are concerned with is in fact *Romeo and Juliet*, how might we approach the opening scene? The scene establishes the conflict between the two houses of Montague and Capulet. It shows the effect of this conflict upon the whole town of Verona. It shows the eruption of the conflict into actual combat. It ends with the intervention of the Prince who imposes a temporary peace by force of arms.

We might approach the scene in five stages:

Stage 1: The Montague-Capulet conflict needs to be seen against the backcloth of the town of Verona. This backcloth we can conveniently create by means of crowd work. We might begin with a fair in the open marketplace, or with a collection of angry citizens met to protest about the continued unrest caused by the two factions. For the sake of argument, let us decide to approach the problem with a market scene. We can begin by arranging stalls, appointing stallholders and involving the rest of the class in buying. When the scene has begun to knit together, we can point out that this is not a simple gathering in a marketplace. Behind the gathering runs the conflict between two very powerful industries on which the life of the town is largely dependent. One produces woollen goods, the other cotton. To an outsider, the conflict seems a little stupid. It would seem possible for the two firms to sink their differences if they would discuss them, and such a sinking would benefit them both. But at the moment, the conflict is very real and at times violent. It divides the town into three groups: those who support one firm, those who support the other, and those who wish to have nothing to do with either. If we encourage discussion in the marketplace, against such a background, it will inevitably become heated.

Stage 2: We now need to particularize the conflict. We can introduce into the generally heated situation, two of the more volatile employees of the wool firm. They could even arrive on motorbikes and sit at the edge of the scene, revving their engines provocatively. They might whistle at the girls and pass loud and derogatory remarks about the older people.

Suppose we now introduce two equally volatile young employees of the cotton firm from the other side of the market-place. They stride into the scene with an arrogant swagger, pick up fruit from a stall and drop it again, comment loudly on the people who get in their way. Then the two pairs see each other. They move round one another like fighting cocks looking for an opening. Only a momentary consideration for the law prevents their striking at once. But even that momentary consideration disappears when both groups see supporters arrive. They begin to fight. Only the intervention of the police brings the fight to an end.

Stage 3: We shall provoke a more lively market scene if we change the climate and the location. 'Fair Verona' would be an appropriate location to change to.

Stage 4: Suppose we put the scene back in time, what would be the effect? The changes need only be superficial. Stallholders will no longer be able to sell pans made of spun aluminium, for example. Instead of a musician playing a violin for coppers, we might have a dancing bear or a trained monkey. If we put the scene back to the sixteenth century, we might have a group of professional tumblers. We can no longer have a conflict between two well-organized industries, but we can preserve the tension and partisanship if we change the industries to politically powerful families. Authority can no longer be represented by the police, but it could certainly be vested in a prince, with a body of retainers.

Stage 5: Already we have more than the bare bones of the opening scene of *Romeo and Juliet*. If we give names to the main participants in the scene—Gregory, Benvolio, Tybalt—we can return to the text. In running through the scene again, using the words of Shakespeare instead of the improvised words that we have had so far, we can make comments that will give the class a deeper insight into the play and at the same time encourage the development of speech. 'John, if you're going to come in as the Prince and stop this fighting at once, you're going to have to speak with a lot more authority.' Comments can also be made in terms of the character, rather than the person playing that character. This allows a child to make considerable adjustments to his speech since he feels that the character shares at least some of the responsibility for his inadequacy: 'Abraham seems a bit tame to me, Edward; can you get him to throw his weight about more?' This approach to the printed text has these virtues:

i   The child is not primarily concerned with words but with those imaginative processes of which the words are simply an outward manifestation. He sees speech—in this case dramatic speech—as being vitally concerned with these inner processes. He sees the printed text as being only the visible tenth of a complex iceberg.

ii   He sees the speeches of the various characters, not as isolated pronouncements, but as the externalization of relationships between those characters. He sees the communicative act of speech as something totally dependent on these relationships. X says 'ii' because Y has said 'i', and because a certain relationship exists between them.

iii   He has an opportunity to practise speech which is limited by the framework created by the dramatist, and yet is wider than his everyday speech inasmuch as the characters are broader than, and different from, his everyday experience.

Group and Individual Work

Speech functions best when a speaker feels no critical pressures upon him. If we tell a child baldly not to drop his 'h's, we start in him, at least as long as we are present, a process of conscious self-criticism that has far more unfortunate effects on his communicative processes than a 'dropped h'. He begins to censor every statement before he finally externalizes it as speech. The result is an interruption in fluency which, if it is carried to its final conclusion, will result in no speech at all. What we are after is not 'correct' speech, but speech; and after that efficient speech.

The principal virtue of crowd work is that no one is watching any particular speaker critically. There is no 'audience factor' since everyone is involved as a participant in the activity. Everyone has the maximum freedom to involve himself totally in the scene, without feeling that he needs to restrict what he is doing and saying to conform to the standards of outside observers. But there are times when it becomes essential to concentrate on the speech needs of a small number of the children present, or even of a single individual. The dramatic approach lends itself very well to speech work with small groups or even individuals.

In the case of a class that is unused to the dramatic approach to speech work, it is better to begin with crowd work that involves them all to start with. From this, small groups or individuals can be withdrawn for particular attention. Suppose we begin with a fairground scene. There are stalls selling cheap trinkets and stalls where pennies are rolled down chutes on to numbered squares. There is a coconut shy and a rifle range. Outside a booth a man is announcing a knife-throwing act that is about to begin. Half a dozen of the crowd are persuaded in. At this point we can stop the scene and point to the booth that few of the others will have noticed:

TEACHER: What d'you think's going on in there?
SYLVIA: It's where somebody throws knives at somebody else.
TEACHER: Have you ever seen it done?
SYLVIA: No.
TEACHER: Well then, let's have a look at what happens inside the booth. Arrange some of the benches across the middle of the floor for the audience to sit on when it comes in. Now this is the inside of the booth. The knife-thrower and his target stand at the front facing each other. We haven't got

a knife-thrower, have we? Richard, take your knives and
go over to that corner; Sylvia, stand facing him. You're the
target. Now, those people who went into the booth, come
and sit down on the benches. Good. Now Arnold, you can
come in from the front of the booth where you were shouting, and announce the act to the audience. . . . The rest
of you just stand clear of the booth.

We have isolated a group with which we propose doing some
more detailed work, and we have put the class into the position
of having to watch without suggesting to them that they are
critical outside observers. They are fellow-workers pausing for
a moment to watch the development of a particular piece of
the total fairground activity. We might work on the scene—
and therefore the speech needs of the scene—like this:

TEACHER: Take it from the beginning again. Arnold, I
want to hear your announcements very clearly from in front
of the booth. You'll have to remember that you're competing
with the other noises—the music from the roundabouts, the
shouts from the coconut shy, the giggles of the people who've
bought funny hats. Then I want to see the audience wondering whether to come into the booth, finally deciding to, then
coming in and sitting down. When they're all in, Arnold,
you'll have to come to the front of them and announce the
act. Then, of course, Richard and Sylvia take up their positions and begin. Now then, Arnold, persuade them to come
in. . . .

Arnold's position is very demanding. It requires a good deal of
volume and at the same time a lot of persuasiveness. He needs
to capture the attention of the passers-by, and then lure them
into the booth by a dramatic account of what they can see
inside for a mere half-crown. Some of his remarks will be
general, some aimed at particular passers-by who are still un-
decided whether to enter or not. If we wished to concentrate
on Arnold's speech, we could do so along these lines. If we
wished to work on the speech of the audience, we could do so
quite easily. Do they know one another? Do they expect some
novel and thrilling experience, or are they blasé from having

been disappointed too many times by side-shows at the fair? Do they complain that they are being kept waiting? How do they react when the knives are thrown?

But suppose that it is Richard and Sylvia on whom we wish to concentrate. They are, after all, the only two whom we have deliberately named for parts not of their own choosing. We might do it like this:

TEACHER: How does it feel, Sylvia, to stand there and have knives thrown at you?

SYLVIA: It's all right.

TEACHER: You've been doing it for a long time, have you?

SYLVIA: Yes—three years.

TEACHER: And he's never missed his aim?

SYLVIA: No.

TEACHER: Well he's going to now.

SYLVIA: Oh, lor!

TEACHER: (*turning to the rest of the class*) Where should the knife land?

MOST: (*if not all*) In the heart! In the throat! In the stomach!

TEACHER: Well if it does, that'll finish the scene, won't it? No, it's just going to graze an arm—this arm nearer the audience. All right, Richard, throw the knife will you?

The knife is thrown. Sylvia reacts. The audience gasps.

TEACHER: Have you missed before, Richard?

RICHARD: No, never.

TEACHER: Not once in three years?

RICHARD: No.

TEACHER: Why did you miss this time?

RICHARD: I was nervous.

TEACHER: What made you nervous?

RICHARD: I don't know.

TEACHER: When you were getting ready for the act, Sylvia, was he nervous then?

SYLVIA: Well—yes, he was a bit.

TEACHER: Did he say why?

SYLVIA: I think he'd been gambling.

99

TEACHER: Gambling! Does he do that much?

SYLVIA: Yes. He's always gambling.

TEACHER: And you don't like it?

SYLVIA: No. It takes all our money. . . .

TEACHER: Look, I think we'd better go back to the dressing-room before the act. Then we might get a better idea of what really happened.

And so we find ourselves not concerned for the moment with a carefree scene at the fair which involves the entire class, but with a human situation between two people that will generate a good deal of feeling:

SYLVIA: You been gambling again?

RICHARD: Mind your own business.

SYLVIA: You're always gambling.

RICHARD: No I'm not.

SYLVIA: Yes you are. . . . How much did you lose this time?

RICHARD: Not much.

SYLVIA: Then why you looking so worried?

RICHARD: I'm not worried.

SYLVIA: Your hand's shaking.

RICHARD: Well?

SYLVIA: I don't like the idea of you throwing knives with a hand like that. . . .

Clearly, the scene between the two of them would justify a lot of time being spent on it. It is likely that it would develop into an open quarrel which would give opportunities for the canalization of strong emotion in speech terms. But we need to remember at this stage that what we are concerned with is not drama as drama, nor drama as a tool for emotional development. We are concerned simply with drama as one of the tools for the development of oral communication skill.

2

An Approach Through Situation

Perhaps the greatest virtue of the dramatic approach to speech development is the fact that it allows a child to experiment with types of oral communication which would otherwise be entirely outside his experience. It allows him, too, to experience a wide range of relationships without which communication cannot take place. But it has a severe disadvantage: whatever we do, the situation remains unconnected with life outside the drama class. We can persuade John, in the capacity of the Prince, to make more noise and show more authority than ever in his life before. But we cannot expect that volume and authority to remain when he becomes John again. He will have had the experience of this additional volume, and he can draw on this experience as John. But he cannot directly transfer the volume necessary for the Prince into the person of John. The phenomenon can be seen at its most marked in the case of some stammerers. William may have an incapacitating stammer in the playground, yet when he assumes the character of Henry V, that stammer might disappear completely. But, as he drops the role of Henry V, the stammer returns as marked as before. It seems that Henry V does not stammer, whereas William does. And between them there is no connection of any sort. William is no more able to 'spill' any of Henry V's fluency into his own speech, than Henry V is able to absorb any of William's stammer.

So the broader speech skill that John has experienced in the drama class, can only be made use of outside it, if we provide him with opportunities for practise in situations which he sees to be part of 'real life'.

And yet this phrase, 'real life', needs a moment's consideration. We cannot engineer many situations within the classroom which are truly 'real life' ones. We can ask a boy to stand up and explain why he has done such an incompetent piece of work on 'The Cotton Industry in Egypt'. This is a 'real life' situation in the sense that it is directly related to the everyday work of the class. But this is not a very useful speech situation. As he stands, he feels thirty pairs of critical eyes upon him. He is expected not to be able to give an adequate explanation; in other words, he knows he is expected to fail. If the situation has any effect on his speech, it will be largely inhibiting. If, on the other hand, we conduct mock interviews with the class, we will find plenty of opportunities for developing speech. But we are at once back to the question, 'Is this a real life situation?' Clearly it is not. There is still an element of 'let's pretend' about it.

And yet there is an important difference between this kind of 'let's pretend' situation and the fully dramatic one. The most important difference is that no characterization is involved.

There is another important difference. A person takes a certain view of himself. He sees certain possibilities before him, however remote they may be. Most boys would see it as just possible that they might be selected to form part of an expedition to the Antarctic. But it is quite outside John's view of possibility to see himself as a Prince in Renaissance Italy. So we can say that whilst most situations that we engineer in the classroom for speech purposes have an element of 'let's pretend' about them, they are 'real life' situations in this sense:

i   The child is involved as himself, not in the guise of some other 'character'.

ii   The child sees the situation as a 'possible' one for him. He sees it as one in which he could well be involved at some later stage of his life. In this sense he sees it as relevant. It is a situation which, though not in itself 'real life', is nonetheless going to prepare him for 'real life'.

Group Question and Answer

We might begin speech work related to particular situations, by forming a panel of experts and asking them questions about their specialist subjects. The panel should consist of five or six children. In a mixed class, the panel should contain both boys and girls. We should brief them, well before the class, on these lines:

> i   Every member of the panel will be expected to pose as an expert in a subject of his own choice. That subject may be History or Geography, Fishing or Football—or anything else. A member would be very unwise to pick a subject about which he knows nothing at all.
> ii   The rest of the class will, in turn, ask the panel a question based on one of these selected subjects. Every member of the panel will have an opportunity to offer some answer, although the fullest and most authoritative answer will be expected from the member whose subject it principally concerns.

As the exercise progresses, we shall find that other considerations emerge. Two or three questioners may call out at the same time from different parts of the class. Two or three members of the panel will begin to answer at the same time. Clearly, someone must be appointed to direct these two things. We shall find that the panel functions best if it is seated on three sides of a table facing the rest of the class. We may wish to take the directing position of Chairman ourselves, in the early stages, but later this can be handed to each member of the panel in turn. We can point out that the function of the Chairman here is to control the proceedings; to select the member of the class who is to put a question, and to select each member of the panel in turn to answer it.

We shall find, as we might expect, that initially questions will be produced by the same few garrulous members of the class. As we proceed, we shall find it necessary to insist on questions from everyone in turn, beginning with the back row and moving forward. We shall have to insist, too, that a questioner speaks effectively enough for his question to be heard and understood by the panel. Some members of the class will see the exercise as an opportunity to trip up the panel by asking questions that they cannot possibly answer. We should point out that, although this can be very useful at a later stage when the panel has sufficient experience to be able to twist any question to its own ends, it is not what is needed at the moment. We are trying to get the panel to talk, not to be rendered speechless. The perfect question is one that gives the panel the maximum opportunity to talk.

The panel itself will very soon realize that it is not sufficient simply to declare itself specialist in half-a-dozen subjects. It must give a good deal of thought to those subjects beforehand if it does not want to reveal its ignorance on elementary points. A specialist in football should at least have been to the trouble to cut out of the paper the table showing the present positions of the teams in the Football League. If he has any views on the playing of football in school, he should have gone to the trouble to jot down a few notes about them on paper. The panel will find, too, that if it is equipped with pencils and rough paper, it can usefully make a note of the main points of a question.

If we look at a good member of the panel, we shall see that this is the result of thought and preparation. It is not simply an accident. Jean, for example, is a good member of the panel. She remembers vividly a holiday she spent some years ago in Scotland, camping with her parents. Last year she went with the school party to Paris. This year she hopes to stay with an aunt in London. She feels she is something of a specialist on travel. But she realizes that her own travel experience is somewhat limited. To fill in the gaps in her knowledge, she has collected pamphlets from a travel agency. She has borrowed a railway timetable from the school office. She has found out the cost of a few selected coach-tours of the Continent. Then she has said to herself: 'What questions would *I* ask a travel expert?' These she has listed:

   i What jobs can a girl do that will give her a chance to travel?

ii What's the cheapest way of travelling?

iii I like the sun and the sea—where should I go?

In the light of questions like these, she has jotted down a few notes on rough paper. These she uses from time to time, as she answers the questions she is asked by the class. Her notes look like this:

Jobs

i Air Hostess—difficult. Need languages. See Youth Employment Officer. Write to airlines—addresses from travel agent.

ii Private Secretary to man who travels. High qualifications. Languages a help. Good shorthand and typing. Well-groomed. Good speech. Watch adverts in Press.

Cheapness

i Hitch-hiking. You need luck. Where are you going to sleep?

ii Cycling. Very good in flat country. Take a tent and a friend. Write to Camping Club.

Sun and Sea

i Italy.

ii Spain.

iii Southern France.

Mountains

i Switzerland.

ii Norway.

Forests

i Sweden.

She uses the information she has collected, like this:

QUESTIONER: My parents won't let me go on the school trip to Rome. What can I say to them?

JEAN: Well—quite a lot. You'll be looked after by teachers, so you'll be as safe as if you were at home. It's not as if you were hitch-hiking. It's very cheap—much cheaper than going by train with your parents. You'll see a lot of Europe— France, Switzerland, Italy and a bit of Germany—and that should broaden your mind. Then you'll hear at least three different languages, and that should help your school work. If you get a job as a private secretary when you leave school, it would be useful if you knew something about other countries. Save your pocket money; that'll show them how keen you are. Mine give me a shilling for cleaning the windows—can't you get yours to do the same?

The questions that members of the class put to the panel are clearly important. A question like, 'What is the first-class air fare from London to Vladivostock?', may be amusing, but it is quite useless. If Jean can answer it she would be better off in a music hall than in school. The best she can hope to do is to tell the questioner to see his travel agent.

A questioner should have some little notice of the specialist subjects that will be represented on the panel, and he should give a little thought to preparing his question. He wants a question that will require a member of the panel to give an extended answer, an answer that requires a certain skill in oral communication. He should ask a question, wherever possible, that arises out of his genuine curiosity and interest. If he has never travelled, has he any interest in how he might start? If he went by train to Bournemouth last year, has he any question about the efficiency of trains? Before finally deciding on his question, he should say to himself, 'If I were on the panel and someone asked me this question, how would I reply?' We can stress the need to ask the right kind of questions, by very occasionally asking the questioner to reply to his own question.

The panel will expect comments on their work. As we have already seen, any comments on speech must be made with care. Since we have been to some trouble to create a situation in which everyone is a participant, for the class is part of the total situation, just as much as the panel, it would be illogical to refuse to allow any member of the situation to make comments. But since it is important that only useful comments be made, we may find it necessary to give the class a framework within which to comment. One way of doing this would be to allow the class to give grades under particular headings to the panel as a whole, for example:

A—a very successful panel.
B—quite a successful panel.
C—the panel needs more experience.

At this stage, comments to individual members of the panel should be restricted to those that encourage.

Individual Question and Answer

The virtue of having children speak as members of a panel, instead of entirely as individuals, is that the responsibility they may feel is shared. If they are not too successful, then this lack of success is not borne entirely by the individual, it is shared by the panel as a whole. We can preserve this valuable panel structure, whilst at the same time concentrating more on the needs of the individual, in this way:

i The panel is still made up of specialists in a wide variety of subjects.

ii There is a chairman whose job it is to control the proceedings. Each member of the panel will fill this position in turn.

iii Each member of the panel in turn gives his opinion on some aspect of his subject.

iv At the end of each opinion, the panel member is asked questions arising out of it by several of the class in turn.

More is demanded of the individual here. Not only must he prepare for any questions that might arise out of his statement, but he must prepare quite specifically for the statement itself. It is important that he understands that it is his *opinion* that is required, not a list of unrelated facts. This would be of little use from a boy who had decided to take Television as his specialist subject:

'In Great Britain there are two kinds of television. One is run by the BBC, the other by the Independent Television Authority. The BBC is paid for out of a licence fee. Independent Television is paid for by advertisers. . . .'

It is a mere regurgitation of facts. It requires no involvement by the boy. It gives no indication that he has absorbed the facts, turned them over in his mind, and come to certain conclusions about them. Speech is a total personality in action; it is not print turned into sound. This would be much more acceptable:

'I like telly. I like the ads. I like that one for sweets where you have a dog that eats them all up and then dad has some more in his pocket. I think there should be more time for ads. They're good. And then there's . . .'

We might be shocked by the opinion, but we cannot deny that it is an opinion. We might be horrified by the muddled way in which that opinion is expressed, but we cannot deny that there is a living human being at work here, doing his best to communicate some of his inner processes to us in terms of speech. This, after all, is what we are trying to develop.

The panel is important here. It must show that interest in what the speaker is saying that will give him a sense of support. He should feel part of the panel, part of a team. He will only feel this if he is convinced that his colleagues are listening to what he is saying, and reacting sympathetically to it. The chairman is important, too. He provides a link with the class and the panel as a whole, as well as a link with the panel and the particular speaker. He should make this link clear by introducing the speaker by name and mentioning, in some quite simple formula, the subject of which the speaker has a specialist knowledge:

'This is Alec Johnson. He's going to give us his views on Poaching. . . .'

The speaker's statement can be very brief. It should do no more than give the class one complete view of an aspect of the subject. He must have given the subject a good deal of previous thought and decided quite clearly what personal view he is going to give. He might find it useful, in trying to arrive at this personal view, to ask himself certain questions: 'Am I in favour of poaching?' 'Do I want the class to take it up?' 'What about poaching other people's ideas—am I in favour of that?'

When he has arrived at a final view, he will find it useful to jot down on rough paper the two or three points he wants to make:

   i   Everyone should try poaching.
   ii It's cheap and exciting.
   iii It gets you out of doors.

These notes will form the basis for a connected, brief statement:

'I went poaching with my brother last week, and I think everyone should try it. It costs very little. Suppose you're after fish; you can make a float, and a hook and line will cost less than sixpence. And it's more exciting than ordinary fishing; you've the excitement of fishing, but you've also the excitement of not being caught. Best of all, it gets you out of the house and into the country. I hope you'll try it.'

The class cannot prepare its questions beforehand. Until the speaker has made his statement, there is no indication of what questions will be relevant. The chairman will have to be sensitive to this fact. He will need to allow the class a few moments in which to formulate questions, before he begins to call for them. He might even remind the class of the gist of what has been said:

'Well, I don't know if we'd all agree with him. He seems very keen on turning us all into poachers. . . .'

Clearly, any comments that the class makes after the exercise, are bound to be more directed towards the performance of individual speakers than to the panel as a whole. We shall need some framework here that produces comments which are useful. A very simple framework that we could easily elaborate as the class became more experienced, would look like this:

Statement

   A—I was quite clear about his views.
   B—I was not quite clear about his views.
   C—He did not really give me any views.

Questions

A—I thought he answered the questions very well.

B—I thought he answered the questions quite well.

C—I think he needs more practice in answering questions.

The class can comment, too, on the questions themselves. They should do so in the light of two considerations:

i   Were the questions relevant to what the speaker had said?

ii   Were they questions which required the speaker to make a connected statement?

The Classroom Interview

The classroom interview does two things:

i   It requires well-organized teamwork from the interviewers.

ii   It places the full responsibility for success or failure upon the person being interviewed.

To be successful, the classroom interview needs careful preparation. Initially, there are virtues in preserving a strong 'let's pretend' factor. Too close an approximation to a 'real life' situation in the early stages, introduces unnecessary and unhelpful stress. What we are after is to give a child experience in presenting himself orally to a small group of others, and expressing himself successfully in response to questions which arise from the situation. Suppose, for example, that we invent a simple road accident that has taken place near the school. We might organize the exercise in these stages:

i   Before the class it will be necessary to organize the teams, each of five or six children, that will conduct the interviews. Three of these will probably be as many as we can handle in one 40-minute period. We shall need to mention certain bald facts:

(a)   The accident took place at the junction of John Street and Sydney Terrace. A small black car struck a schoolboy as he was crossing the road.

(b)   The time was 12.30 p.m.

(c)   The person being interviewed is the driver of the car.

ii   The interview is being conducted by a team from the school. Their purpose is to find out what really happened, so that they can suggest how it can be avoided in the future. We should avoid having a team of police interrogators, unless the class is experienced. Such interrogators might find it irresistible to hide behind crude caricatures of policemen of the 'hello, hello—what have we here?' type.

iii   Ideally, the interview should be conducted in the centre of the room, with all participants seated at a large table. In many classrooms there will be physical reasons which make this impossible. In that case, the group should be seated at the front of the class.

iv   A chairman will be required to control the proceedings. The team members will each fill the positions of chairman and interviewee in turn.

The interviewers must agree beforehand on the kind of information they want. Do they consider it important to know the speed of the car and the weather conditions? Do they want to know how long the driver has been driving? The interviewee, too, will need to have given his side of the picture some thought. He will need to know exactly where the accident took place; he will have to have made up his mind about the cause and where the responsibility lies.

The class is in a new position. It is no longer an integral part of the proceedings. The interviews could take place without the class altogether. At best, the class is a group of interested observers. This might bring new difficulties. If the interviews are dull, will the class continue to sit in cooperative silence? If an interviewee can be heard by the interviewers, but not by the rest of the class, can the class legitimately complain? And yet, when it comes to making comments on the work of the team, the class is in the best position to do so. We might use a form of comment like this:

Interviewers

Preparation for the Interview
  A—Good.
  B—Adequate.
  C—Insufficient.

Conduct of the Interview
  A—The interviewee was given a very good chance to explain himself. The interviewers got all the necessary information from him.
  B—The interviewee was given a fair chance to explain himself. The interviewers got most of the necessary information from him.
  C—The interviewee was not encouraged to explain himself. The interviewers got little of the necessary information from him.

Interviewee

Preparation for the Interview
  A—Good.
  B—Adequate.
  C—Insufficient.

Response to Questions
  A—The interviewee put his case clearly and well.
  B—The interviewee was quite good in putting his case.
  C—The interviewee did not put his case very well.

Any assessment made by the class can be accompanied by examples. Anything that is said should be framed in such a way that it can be made use of by the people to whom it is addressed.

We can twist the situation by having one interviewer and a number of interviewees. The interviewer might be an employee of a television company, asked to cover the accident for a news broadcast. The interviewees might be witnesses or local shop-keepers. One might be a parent or a brother of the injured boy. The interviewer would have to prepare his line of questioning very carefully. Each interviewee would have to decide what his relationship was with the accident.

The interview situation can be varied considerably. The numbers of people involved can be varied. The 'let's pretend' element can be varied to the point where it almost ceases to exist. An interview, for example, conducted to select a class monitor, would have no 'let's pretend' quality about it at all.

The Outside Interview

With very rare exceptions, the Classroom Interview has a marked 'let's pretend' element. Nothing is finally at stake. To progress towards speech that is successful for 'real life' purposes, we must produce situations which are themselves 'real life'. The Outside Interview can provide such situations, where the interview is not an end in itself but a valuable tool towards achieving some other end. For example, we might wish to conduct a local social survey; the end would be the survey itself, but the tool would be the interview. We might conduct such a survey in six stages:

i   A clear statement of the terms of reference.
ii   Full preparation for the kind of things we wish to find out.
iii   The choice of teams and rehearsals.
iv   The conduct of the survey in the field.
v   The report back to the class.
vi   The final conclusion of the class.

As an example of how these stages would work in a particular case, let us examine them in more detail:

i   Terms of reference

We can begin by asking the class what they think of a newspaper heading that reads, 'ALL SUCCESSFUL PEOPLE RUDE AND RUTHLESS—SAYS VICAR', and a quotation below it, " 'I've never met a successful person who wasn't both rude and ruthless," said the Rev. James Cargill, at a garden party yesterday. This could form the basis for a local survey, designed to discover whether the statement had any truth in it, as far as the class could discover. We should explain that we will draw up a list of local people whom we consider successful in their various fields, and interview them. If the interviews are carried out carefully, we should have the necessary material against which to test the vicar's statement.

We shall need to define the words, 'successful', 'rude' and 'ruthless'. We might consider whether it would be worth interviewing an 'unsuccessful' person. It might also be worth hearing the opinion of a vicar.

The terms of reference might be stated like this:

'To find out, by personal interview, whether it is true that all successful people are rude and ruthless.'

ii *Preparation*

Careful preparation is vital for the success of such a project. We shall need to find out, for example, these things:

i The background of the person being interviewed. It might be significant to know whether he achieved success or was born to it. It might be significant, too, to know his age.
ii The views of the person on the statement, 'All successful people are rude and ruthless.'
iii The views of the person on how success is achieved.

Before we work out lists of questions, we must decide on the interviewees and how they are to be approached to grant an interview. Although the questions will be designed to find out the same things about each person to be interviewed, the kind of person we imagine him to be will to some extent affect the approach and the actual wording of the questions. It is possible to ask the age of a successful pigeon-breeder in his early teens; it would be disastrous to do so of an actress in her forties.

The kind of person to be interviewed will also dictate to some extent the best way in which they might be initially approached. Would it be better, for example, to make the initial approach to a successful headmaster directly by telephone or less directly by letter? How much detail of exactly what we are doing do we need to explain to him initially? Whatever our conclusions on these points, the interviewers themselves must finally make the approach, since this approach is an essential part of the total situation.

iii *Teams and Rehearsal*

If we divide a class of thirty children into interviewing groups of three, we shall have a good deal of information on ten successful people. This information should be sufficient to allow the class to draw firm conclusions about the initial statement. When the teams have been selected, they should be asked to prepare a list of questions that will provide information on the necessary points. They should decide, too, which member of the team is to ask which questions, and in what order. They should realize that however carefully the questions have been prepared, they can never be regarded as finally fixed. They must always remain no more than reminders of the line of questioning that is necessary, since speech is affected fundamentally by the situation in which it is being used and however much information we collect beforehand on a particular interviewee we can never predict exactly what the total situation will be like when the interviewers finally confront him. We might decide, for example, that it would be significant to find out whether good health is related to success. A successful person who is an invalid, for example, might be rude, not because he is successful but because he is an invalid. In preparing for the interview it might seem very reasonable to plan to pose the question, 'Have you ever been ill?' But suppose that when the interviewers arrive, they are shown into a sick room where the interviewee, too kind to cancel the interview, is huddled in a chair recovering from influenza. The question, asked in the form in which it had been planned, could lead to their being promptly shown out again. All questions, they must be reminded, may have to be adjusted in the light of the total situation in which they find themselves.

One important feature that cannot be discovered by any

direct question is the impression of rudeness or otherwise that the interviewers get of the person they interview. They will need to be reminded that their own personal impressions are extremely important. They will need to write down notes about them as soon as they leave the interviewee's presence. The class will certainly attach importance to these impressions. They will need to be carefully and fairly made.

Some rehearsal of the interview by each team will be necessary. They must be clear which of them is to make the introductory statement about what they are doing, and who is to begin the questioning. These rehearsals can be conducted as a 'let's pretend' situation, with other members of the class playing the role of interviewee. One of the team will need to check the time involved in the rehearsed interview, since, however cooperative a successful man might be, he cannot be expected to submit to an interview for too long.

iv *Conduct in the Field*

The actual conduct of the interview will be important, since it can affect the information that the teams are trying to collect. The personal behaviour of the teams will be important. They need to be as pleasant and cooperative as possible. If they are not, then this might make the interviewee's brusqueness quite justified.

Their equipment should be minimal. They should have only well-sharpened pencils and their question papers. Beside each question should be sufficient space to jot down a note or two from which they can write down the full answer immediately after the interview. At the top of the question paper they should have the name of the interviewee, the title of his job and any brief personal notes they think might be useful for the conduct of the interview. They should be reminded that since they are unlikely to be able to rest their papers on a table, they will have to write with the papers on their knees. This can be very difficult. They would find it easier to have their questions and spaces for the answers, in an exercise book.

v *The Report Back*

The report back to the class should be oral. Each member of each team should organize the answers to the questions in such a way that he can use them to make a brief statement of his findings. He should organize his total impressions of the interviewee as well, and tell the class what they amount to. He should be prepared to answer any questions put to him by members of the class who wish a particular point to be clarified.

The class will need to make sufficient rough notes on each statement to be able to recall its main points when the time comes for a final judgment. It should also be asked to give an assessment on the success with which each team has done its job.

vi *The Final Conclusion*

The class should now be asked to come to a conclusion on the original statement, 'All successful people are rude and ruthless.' It will have to bear in mind all the information that has been collected and all the personal impressions that have been voiced. Discussion might be necessary to unravel one or two remaining problems and the final decision might have to be taken by a show of hands.

There is a temptation to think of this stage as being somewhat irrelevant. The real body of work has been completed. Everyone in the class has had personal experience of the Outside Interview and that was the real intention of the project. True, the class has been asked to make a judgment on the facts that it has collected, and such an ability to judge is regarded as having a certain educational value. But the judgment seems a little unconnected with the process of speech development.

Yet in a sense, this final stage is the most important of the exercise. It is the logical endproduct that turns the exercise from yet another 'let's pretend' activity into a 'real life' situation. To go out and interview successful adults in their homes and offices for no good reason, is an activity with a high degree of unreality about it. But to interview them for some prepared and reasonable purpose, changes the nature of the activity. It becomes significant. It becomes 'real life'.

The Outside Interview was employed by day-release students at the Lyons Student Centre, Hammersmith Day College, to produce a publication, *The Interviewers*.[1] They describe their approach in an editorial:

'We suggest names and search for addresses, write letters, type the corrected version, sign and send them off; then we await replies—receive friendly regrets with interest and appreciation, but acceptances with rejoicing; we settle time and place to suit the subject—often by telephone—then decide who are to do the interview, sharing out the experiences, and, if necessary, drawing lots; we prepare the questions, sometimes after some research, and present ourselves at the meeting place, maybe at our Student Centre or even as far as Elstree Film Studios; we conduct the interview, make notes or do a tape recording, ask for a photograph. write up the report and type the corrected copy.'[2]

The Formal Statement

The Interview gives an opportunity for children to talk *in association with* others, within the framework of a given situation. But there are times when people find it necessary to talk *to* others in a more formal and extended way. The teacher does this. The lecturer and politician do this. It is a skill required of the shop-steward, the union leader, the lawyer, the salesman, the priest. Since this situation is so common in life outside the classroom, the school-leaver should at least have had some experience of it.

Preparation for the interview is limited. Its nature cannot be predicted in detail. But detailed preparation for the formal statement is not only possible but essential. Two questions arise:

i   What will the formal statement allow a speaker to do?
ii   What kind of preparation is necessary?

[1] 'Way to the Stars', *The Times Educational Supplement*, 15 May 1964.
[2] *The Interviewers*, Vol. 2. Lyons Student Centre.

The formal statement allows a speaker to give his views—his opinions—at some length. It allows him to use arguments in support of those views and to answer those arguments against them. It allows him to make recommendations that arise out of his views. In preparing this statement, then, it will be necessary for the speaker to find answers to four general questions:

i What am I hoping to achieve by talking to this group of listeners?
ii What effective arguments can I find that will support my case?
iii What are the arguments against my case likely to be, and how can I answer them?
iv What recommendations do I wish to make to the listeners?

Let us consider how this shape might be used to handle a particular situation. Suppose the situation is this: During its passage through the lower forms of the school, this class that we are now teaching has been accustomed to a one-day outing during the summer term. The outing has been to some local site of historical interest. This year the outing for the class has been cancelled, because of the increased pressure of examination work. If we face a child with this situation and ask for his views on it, he might begin his preparation by giving more specific answers to the four general questions:

i What am I hoping to achieve? I want the school to reconsider its decision. I'd like it to reverse it. At least it might find a compromise solution.
ii Arguments supporting me:
    (a) The outing has educational value.
    (b) A relaxation from school work.
iii Arguments against me: need to concentrate on exams.
    Answer: Are they everything in a school?
iv Recommendations:
    (a) School should think again.
    (b) Can't we compromise? Why not go on a Saturday?
A child who has gone through this process has begun to

organize his ideas to meet the demands of a particular situation. He now needs to clarify and develop those ideas so that when he stands in front of the class he is able to make a coherent and relevant statement. In the process of clarification, many of his original ideas will remain; but a few will inevitably be changed as he sees a better argument or a better way of putting an existing argument. His notes resulting from this process of clarification, might look like this:

  i Problem: cancellation of outing because of exams. News came as shock to all. Is there no other way out?

  ii Two points:

    (a) Educational value: I'm doing History this year, and I've never seen a medieval castle. There's one at Blank. If I went there with a teacher he could explain it to me.

    (b) Relaxation. Particularly necessary in a year where exams are so important.

  iii We need to concentrate on exams. Of course, but isn't a school supposed to do more than this?

  iv I recommend:

    (a) That we agree to an extra half-hour of homework this term;

    (b) That we ask the school to allow us the one-day outing;

    (c) That we sign a petition (I must have this prepared) and take it to the headmaster.

This is no doubt a fairly sophisticated child in a fairly democratic school, but the basic approach can be similar to this whatever the age of the child and whatever the situation out of which his statement arises.

Preparation is essentially these things:

  i The perception of the total situation.

  ii An attitude towards that situation.

  iii The organization of mental processes to which that attitude gives rise.

  iv The formulation of those organized processes in oral terms.

This process has nothing to do with written language, as such. In consequence, it would be as well not to encourage the child to write his statement out in the form of connected written language and get him to read it to the class. It is not true that written and spoken language are totally different, but it is a good working premise for educational purposes. Much of the effectiveness of the child's case will be dependent upon the immediacy of his contact with his listeners. To place a sheet of paper between him and the listeners will only add to his difficulties.

It is useful if he is questioned on his statement by members of the class. It is, in any case, a logical finale to what the speaker has said. He has had an opportunity to put a personal view to the listeners, without their interrupting him. If they disagree with him, it is only reasonable that they should be given some opportunity to interrogate him on one or two points. The speaker's ability to stand up to such interrogation is part of his ability to make a formal statement.

The class might make an assessment of what he has done on this basis:

A—I agree with all his recommendations.

B—I agree with some of his recommendations.

C—I agree with none of his recommendations.

If some of the class give an assessment of 'C', they will need to make a further assessment:

A—I understand all his recommendations very clearly, but I can't support them.

B—I understood some of his recommendations; others I didn't follow.

C—I really had difficulty in deciding what it was he was recommending.

3

An Approach Through Reading

Reading, of course, means reading aloud. This seems self-evident. But it is necessary to repeat it because of the view that is still held that silent reading is a sufficient preparation for reading aloud. There seems no reason for supposing that silent reading and silent comprehension have any relation at all with speech skill.[1] Indeed, what transference there is from one of these activities to the other, seems all to be from speech to silent reading.[2]

The principal virtue of reading aloud as a tool for speech development is this: speech requires the generation and organization of mental processes and their externalization as complex movement; reading aloud gives us an opportunity to concentrate on the second part of this process, since the material necessary for the first part is provided by the reading passage. Reading aloud gives us an opportunity for developing such external factors of the total speech process as Volume, Articulation and Flexibility. It gives us an opportunity, too, to develop any interpretative skills with which we consider we should be concerned.

Suppose we ask a child to prepare a short prose passage with a view to reading it aloud to the class. This might be a useful passage for the purpose:

[1] 'Speech Education'; *The Times Educational Supplement,* 22 June 1962.

[2] Edfeldt, A. W.: *Silent Speech and Silent Reading,* Almqvist and Wiksell, Stockholm, 1959.

TRANSPORT PROBLEMS

Broadly speaking, there are just two methods of getting yourself about the country independently when you are on holiday: on foot and on wheels.

If you are on foot you will cover shorter distances, but you will get to know the places you visit better because it will take you longer to pass through them and as you walk you will have plenty of time to look around you. If you go on wheels, under your own power or motorized, you will be able to travel farther and more quickly, and of course to carry more with you. The choice really depends first on your resources, second on your inclination.

Travelling on foot, another great advantage is that you can go wherever the fancy takes you. For you, all roads are through roads, including the many footpaths which run from village to village all over Britain. In unfenced country, you can take to the hills if you wish and no questions will be asked so long as you do no damage; among fenced fields and woods, you should always ask permission to tramp over the land if you can find out who the owner is, and having got permission you must be careful to shut gates after you, leave no litter and do no damage to cattle or crops, and respect any 'private, keep out' notices you may see.

On fairly easy ground twenty miles a day is a reasonable distance for a walker to cover; on rough or hilly ground, ten miles a day is plenty. Do not rush: find the pace that suits you best, and stick to it. Some walkers recommend taking a rest of about ten minutes in each hour, others keep going for two or three hours and then take a longer break.

PAMELA CARMICHAEL, *Modern Living: Your Holidays,*
Longmans 1963.

Uncomplicated passages of this sort are essential initially. We are concerned principally with the technical aspects of communication. To give a child a passage which makes great demands on his understanding and interpretative ability, is to complicate unnecessarily an already quite complicated situation.

We can help the reader to define the situation for himself by asking the class what effect he had upon them. We should be strict in excluding any comment from them that is not related to the question, 'Was he producing enough volume for this situation?' The comment, 'He was mumbling,' should be disallowed. If it means anything to the reader, it is a comment on his articulation not his volume. The comment, 'He sounded very sad when he was talking about walking from village to village,' is irrelevant too. It refers to interpretation, not to volume. On the other hand the comment, 'I could hardly hear him,' is highly relevant. It refers directly to the fact that he was not making enough noise. A simple assessment scheme might keep the class's mind on its job of listening, and at the same time provide the reader with a useful indication of his success or failure. This might be sufficient:

A—I can hear him very well.
B—I can hear him quite well.
C—I cannot hear him very well.

We can tackle this problem of defining the situation by asking everyone in the class to raise a hand. Hands should be lowered when the volume has reached a level that the individual listener finds satisfactory. The reader might deal with the problem in stages, concentrating his attention on the front row until all hands have disappeared, and then extending his attention to the next row. This will require that he keeps some visual contact with the class, and this in itself raises a new consideration, linked with, but different from, volume.

Relationships

Communication cannot take place unless a relationship exists between speaker and listener. Part of a reader's difficulty is that he does not know what is being expected of him. He thinks, when he is asked to read aloud, that it is sufficient to turn print into sound. He does not appreciate that what is required of him is a communicative act. Such an act requires the establishment of a relationship between himself and the listeners. When he is forced to keep a visual check on the raised hands in front of him, he is beginning to establish this relationship. The hands belong to people. They will not be lowered until the people are satisfied. The visual contact does not of itself constitute a relationship, but it is a sound beginning for one. He will begin to see that what is required is not for him to read aloud in the presence of other people, but to read *to* other people; and before he can read to them he must at least become aware of their existence.

A simple form of assessment that the class might use here, would be this:

A—He is reading to us all the time.
B—He is reading to us some of the time.
C—He is not really reading to us.

Articulation

Volume and a relationship are fundamental. So is an articulatory process that is sufficiently precise as to leave the listener in no doubt concerning the speaker's meaning.

We could explain to the class that the next step was to make sure that they could *understand* everything that was being read to them. They would see what was required of them if we asked them to make an assessment on these lines:

A—I could understand everything he was saying.
B—I could understand a good deal of what he was saying.
C—I could understand very little of what he was saying.

We can help, of course, with this process by choosing a reading passage that requires a good deal of rather precise articulation. A passage full of facts might provide a good example. If the facts are not clearly presented to the listeners, they cannot be expected to understand the passage. It can occasionally be helpful, too, if we tell the reader that what we are concerned with is not sufficient articulatory movement, but an excess of it: 'Go on, Christopher,' we might feel inclined to say. 'Just for once, overdo it.' It will be quite incredible if he succeeds. The social pressure against his doing so is almost insurmountable. But he might be persuaded to do it 'a little more'. That 'little more' might be enough to make him quite understandable.

The 'let's pretend' approach has its limitations, as we have seen. But it might be worth experimenting with the suggestion that he is reading to a class of hard-of-hearing children. To get in touch with them, what he needs is not any increase in volume, but an increase in articulatory movement.

There is one hazard that we will inevitably encounter. It is the tendency for the reader to dispense with all continuity and give us simply one word—or even one sound—after another:

'The—pause—man—pause—ran—pause—after—pause—the pause—dog.'

This is a useless activity. It has nothing to do with speech. We should point out that speech is a continuity, not a string of isolated sounds:

TEACHER: Wait a bit, wait a bit. I think he's dodging the issue, don't you? What was he doing then?
JOHN: Just one word after another.
TEACHER: What's wrong with that?
JOHN: It's not speaking.
TEACHER: Not speaking, isn't it? Well what's speaking then?
BETTY: Speaking; well, it—like flows. . . .
TEACHER: Of course. If you chop it up into little bits it isn't speaking any longer. Speech is like water from a hosepipe. You've turned it into icecubes. All right, Christopher; thaw it out again. . . .

Speed

Most children read too quickly. As much as anything, the cause is a failure to establish the right relationship with the listeners. They do not appreciate the needs of the listeners. It will be necessary to point out to them that there are two kinds of speed:

i The speed at which a shorthand specialist can record what is being said.

ii The speed at which a listener can take in *and understand* what is being said.

A listener is expected to do far more than a shorthand specialist. He is expected to receive the speech, perceive the meaning, and make sense of that meaning by referring it to what he already knows. To do this he needs time. The newer the material, the more complex the argument, the more time the listener needs. From the speaker's point of view there is another consideration. There is a speed beyond which it is no longer possible to move human flesh and bone accurately. A tennis player can return balls thrown to him over the net at five-second intervals, but he cannot return balls that reach him at half-second intervals, because it is not in the nature of the human arm to move with accuracy at that speed. The same is true of speech. Beyond a certain speed, it is no longer possible for the human articulatory mechanism to move with the accuracy necessary to produce understandable speech. For this reason, excessive speed is usually accompanied by articulatory imprecision.

Putting reading aside for a moment, we might ask the question, 'Why do some people speak so quickly that it is difficult to follow them?' We must remember that speech is two things: mental activity and the externalization of that activity in movement terms. To say to a person, 'Slow down' or 'You speak too quickly', is not necessarily helpful. The person is likely to interpret such a comment as referring only to the second part of speech—the rate of movement of the articulatory mechanism. But part of the difficulty is the rate of generation of ideas. If he succeeds in slowing down the physical side of speech without slowing down the rate at which he is generating those ideas that he is trying to externalize as sound, he will be in a worse state than he was before our comment. He will have reduced the size of the channel of communication, without having reduced the material he is trying to cram through that channel. He will, as it were, have a backlog of mental activity that he cannot externalize as sound because he thinks we have placed restrictions on the use of the technical side of the process. What seems to be necessary is not to slow down the rate of speech, but the rate of generation of those ideas he is turning into speech. This is usually best done, not by commenting on the speed at which he is speaking, but by defining for him more clearly the situation in which he is using speech.

Suppose we take a reading passage that is dependent upon a closely argued case. That case is argued by the inclusion of a number of facts. If these facts are not grasped by the listener, the argument will mean nothing to him. To grasp these facts the listener needs time. If he were allowed to, he might want to say after each fact, 'Hang on a minute—"Robert Earl Hughes weighed 76 stone 5 pounds"—good heavens, that's about seven times what I weigh! What a size!—— Yes, all right; I've got that. You can carry on now.' Since the listener cannot be allowed to make such comments out loud, the reader will have to imagine what is going on in the listener's head, and allow for that process in his reading. This requires a close relationship with the listener. A relationship that allows the reader to be sensitive to the listener's needs. In the initial stages of reading such material, the reader might actually mark on the reading passage the facts that are crucial. He will need to present these with absolute clarity and he will need to 'hang on a minute' after each of them and check by a glance at the listeners that the fact has not only reached them but has been grasped. He might even say to himself as he looks at the listeners, 'Well now, have you got that?'

The class might make an assessment on these lines:

A—This speed is all right for me.
B—I'd like him to be a bit faster.
C—I'd like him to be a bit slower.

We might find it useful to suggest to a reader that he should try as an experiment to read *too* slowly. It is very unlikely that he will be successful. In this case the class might make an assessment on these lines:

A—I'd like him to be a bit faster.
B—This speed is all right for me.
C—I'd like him to be still slower.

As with the work for increased articulatory precision, we should insist here on the continuity of speech. To break up connected speech into single words separated by long pauses, is not to slow down speech but to destroy its essence.

Interpretation

We would be ignoring the full possibilities of reading as a tool for speech education, if we were to treat it simply as a way of developing the external aspects of speech. It can be used, too, for the development of those processes out of which these external aspects arise.

Interpretation requires these things:
i   A full understanding of the author's intention.
ii   A relationship with a listener.
iii   An ability to communicate that intention to that listener in terms of voice and speech.

The word 'understanding' needs a little explanation. A correct answer to the question, 'What does the author mean by . . . ?' shows understanding. A good answer to the question, 'Comment on the author's use of humour in the passage', shows understanding. But it is understanding of a kind. It is not necessarily that total understanding essential for interpretation. Obviously the reader must understand 'what the author means by . . .' But whereas it is possible to sit morosely at an examination desk and write satisfactory comments on the author's use of humour, it is not possible to stand morosely and read the passage to the class with any hope of success. Interpretation demands total involvement with the author's intention. A reader must not only understand the author's use of humour, he must be actively amused by it. And it is this active amusement that he must communicate, not his own intellectual comments on it. To communicate anger the reader must become angry. The interpreter does not stay outside the situation, he becomes the situation. We need to appreciate the difference here between the critical view and the interpretative. The critic can remain uninvolved with the situation and talk about it to us; the interpreter, by becoming totally involved in the situa-

F

tion, can show it to us. The reader of a humorous passage is not required to tell us about humour, he is required to show humour to us in action.

We might begin with an uncomplicated passage like this:

SHARK

In reality the whale shark went on encircling us for barely an hour, but to us the visit seemed to last a whole day. At last it became too exciting for Erik, who was standing at a corner of the raft with an eight-foot hand harpoon, and encouraged by ill-considered shouts, he raised the harpoon above his head. As the whale shark came gliding slowly towards him, and had got its broad head right under the corner of the raft, Erik thrust the harpoon with all his giant strength down between his legs and deep into the whale shark's gristly head. It was a second or two before the giant understood properly what was happening. Then in a flash the placid half-wit was transformed into a mountain of steel muscles. We heard a swishing noise as the harpoon line rushed over the edge of the raft, and saw a cascade of water as the giant stood on its head and plunged down into the depths. The three men who were standing nearest were flung about the place head over heels, and two of them were flayed and burnt by the line as it rushed through the air. The thick line, strong enough to hold a boat, was caught up on the side of the raft but snapped at once like a piece of twine, and a few seconds later a broken-off harpoon shaft came up to the surface two hundred yards away. A shoal of frightened pilot fish shot off through the water in a desperate attempt to keep with their old lord and master, and we waited a long time for the monster to come racing back like an infuriated submarine; but we never saw anything more of the whale shark.

THOR HEYERDAHL, *The Kon-Tiki Expedition*,
Allen & Unwin, 1950.

The passage reports an incident at sea. It is exciting. It is dramatic. It has considerable tension, particularly towards the end. Any successful interpretation must present all these things. The reader is required not merely to 'understand' the excitement and tension; he is required to feel them, and then to communicate that feeling.

If we think it useful for the listeners to make individual judgments on what the reader has done, we might suggest this to them as a formula:

A—The reader got the meaning of the passage across to me very well.

B—He got the meaning across fairly well.

C—He didn't really get the meaning across.

A more complex passage would be this:

THE ROAD TO ROME

When the battle had been raging for nearly a fortnight, Simon sent for Angelo and said to him in a casual way, 'We are going to have a little party on our own. There is a rumour that the Germans are about to do something that we take a poor view of, and I'm going to see if I can put a stop to it. It will be quite a small party, but I've got permission to take you with us. You will be very useful, knowing your way about Rome as you do, and I thought you might like to come. We start tomorrow.'

'And where is your party going to be?' asked Angelo.

'In Rome,' said Simon. 'Didn't I make that clear?'

'But Rome is still occupied by the Germans!'

'That will add to the interest of it, don't you think?——Why, what's the matter?'

Before Simon could catch him, Angelo fell to the ground in a dead faint. Simon made haste to turn him over, to loosen his belt, to pour water on his face and chafe his hands. As soon as he showed signs of recovery, Simon gave him rum in an enamel mug, and Angelo sat up, pale and shivering.

'What is the matter?' Simon repeated with anxiety in his voice. 'Are you ill?'

Angelo stared at him with wide-open, terrified eyes. Never in his life had he heard a more fearful proposal. The shock of hearing it had frightened the blood from his brain.

ERIC LINKLATER, Private Angelo, Cape, 1946.

The added complication here arises, of course, from the introduction of dialogue. Dialogue is spoken by a person and a person has certain characteristics. These characteristics are an essential part of the author's total intention. They need to be communicated by the reader. The listener needs to be shown the nature of the character who is speaking the words. Here again, the problem for the reader is one of involving himself with the character. It is not enough for him to know that a particular character is old and rude; he must present an old, rude person to the listener.

All interpretative work presupposes an ability to communicate. We have seen some of the factors on which successful oral communication is dependent. However involved we find ourselves becoming in the problems of interpretation, it is essential that we keep a check from time to time on such factors as volume, articulation, speed, and the nature of the relationship between reader and listener.

Choice of Reading Material

Reading passages can be chosen so as to set particular problems for the reader. One passage might demand considerable volume, another considerable articulatory skill. But for whatever purpose we choose a passage, we should bear in mind one question: 'Can this passage be read aloud by children of this age-group in the classroom situation?' Such a question will exclude much material that is regarded as great literature, and include much that we think worthless from a literary point of view. But we are not principally concerned here with the literary value of written language. We are concerned with the development of fluent speech processes.[1]

[1] For a more detailed practical approach to reading, see Wise, *Reading and Talking in English*, Harrap, 1964.

4

An Approach
Through Mechanical Aids

Increasingly, mechanical aids which are available in school can
be of value in speech education. Language laboratories are
appearing in schools. Whilst at the moment they are designed
to be used in connection with studies in a foreign language,
experience may show that they might have some application
to speech education. The use of closed-circuit television is not
beyond the experimental stage, but it too has possibilities that
could be of value in the development of speech communication
processes.

The Tape Recorder

The principal piece of apparatus now in general use in schools,
is the tape recorder. It can be very valuable, but like all
mechanical apparatus it has quite severe limitations. It is
popularly thought to be almost the badge of the speech educationist, as popular television programmes suggest that the
stethoscope is the badge of the doctor. This attitude to the
tape recorder has found its way even into some schools. 'We're
hoping to begin speech work next year, when the Authority
buys us a tape recorder,' can be heard rather too frequently. It
suggests that the machine is indispensable to speech development. This is so mistaken an idea of what is involved in speech
education, that it justifies a more detailed look at the limitations and possibilities of an invention that at times, and under

certain circumstances, can be a quite useful tool in speech development.

Limitations

The limitations of the tape recorder are very severe. In the first place it may cost anything from £50 to £120, and in addition there will be certain maintenance costs. Schools, forever it seems on restricted budgets, may find it difficult to justify such a sum of money when there are so many more important and urgent calls on their funds. In the second place, to be of real value the machine must be freely available for any member of staff to use in the course of any lesson that might appear to benefit from its use. This presupposes the unlikely luxury of having one room in the school specifically set aside for classes that involve the recording of speech, or the play-back of pre-recorded speech. The alternative is to carry the machine from one room to another, as it is required. The weight of some machines is so great that this involves very considerable effort, even for a strong and healthy male.

But, even supposing that the cost is no problem and that a technique is evolved for moving the machine easily and quickly from one part of the school to another, there remains the question, 'What are we to do with it when it is set up?' We must remind ourselves of the view we are taking of speech, a view that sees speech as a piece of total human behaviour, involving complex psychological processes, living relationships, and complicated movement. The machine inevitably disregards the visual aspects of human communication, and we have seen that this is an integral part of the speech process. It will not reproduce the nature of the relationship that must exist between speaker and listener, and this too is an integral part of speech as communication. It does not necessarily reproduce voice quality with sufficient fidelity for our purposes; as we have seen, voice quality is a highly significant aspect of the total communication process.

An experiment with the apparatus will reveal another limitation. If we speak into the microphone from the distance of a foot, the play-back will give an impression of immediacy. If we step back three feet and speak again at the same volume, the play-back gives an impression of distance far in excess of the actual distance involved. It gives the listener an impression of the speaker having been removed from him, of being remote. It gives an impression, too, of a considerable drop in volume. We can demonstrate this further by putting a microphone at the back of a classroom in an attempt to record the impression of a teacher's speech formed by a child on the back row. If we sit on the back row ourselves, we shall have our own 'live' impression of the teacher's speech to compare with that that the machine will shortly reproduce. These may be some of the impressions that we form of the situation before we hear the play-back:

i   The teacher's speech is loud enough and precise enough. It communicates well. He stops speaking when he writes on the board. He stops occasionally to glance round the room to check that everyone is following what he is saying.

ii   Two children on the back row whisper together for a moment. They are so quiet that no one appears to notice them. Another child taps a pencil very gently on the top of his desk. He happens to be sitting next to the microphone. None of these acts in any way affects the power and continuity of the teaching.

On the play-back, the impression will be totally different. We shall hear every syllable of the two whispering children. The tapping pencil will sound like a bass drum. All the coughs and shuffles of the class, that never reached our consciousness in the 'live' situation, will be faithfully reproduced. Apparently from some far part of the school, we will just be able to hear the voice of the teacher. We will realize at once that although in a sense it is an accurate reproduction of the situation in terms of sound, it has nothing at all to do with the situation that we actually witnessed.

This distortion of volume and distance is important when we come to use the machine in class for the purposes of speech development. If, for example, we have two children, Brenda, a loud and ebullient girl, and Terence, a quiet and withdrawn boy. We might think that for Terence to read a scene from a play with Brenda, might have the effect of drawing him out a little. In theory it well might. Suppose we decide to play the scene into a microphone so that afterwards we can say to Terence, 'There now, Terence; that's a lot better, isn't it?' That will give him confidence to communicate with a little more strength, and his further success will give him further confidence. But suppose we overlook this particular limitation of the apparatus and let Brenda stand a foot away from the microphone whilst Terence is three feet from it. The result on play-back will do anything but give Terence increased confidence. Instead of sounding rather quiet, he will sound infinitesimal. Brenda, on the other hand, may seem to be dominating the whole room. The result will be to demonstrate in public that the machine does not think that Terence compares very favourably with Brenda. If our intention is to give Terence the confidence to make more noise, we would be better cheating by placing him next to the microphone and drawing Brenda away from it.

There is a not uncommon view of a recording machine that implies that the very possession of one has some beneficial effect on speech development. These are authentic remarks made by teachers, training college lecturers and lecturers in university departments of education:

> 'His speech is very poor. Hasn't he heard himself on tape?'
> 'Yes, we've got a tape recorder at last. Now we can get down to this business of speech education.'
> 'I agree, his speech is awful. But we've a tape recorder in the department—you'd think he'd take the trouble to use it.'
> 'First thing we do here is put all our people on tape. Then they know what they've got to do.'

But to have a tape recorder that will reproduce with the highest fidelity the sound that has been put into it, is not enough. We need as well an ability to hear the sound that is reproduced and an ability to make critical *and useful* judgments upon it. It seems that as far as speech goes the last person who is able to do this is the person responsible for that speech. A person who hears his speech reproduced by a recorder for the first time, is likely to make remarks like these:

> 'But that's not me, is it? I mean, it doesn't sound at all like me. I'd no idea my voice was so high-pitched; and that awful Cockney accent . . . !'

None of these remarks is very useful, nor, when we come to try to relate them to the actual recording, is any very accurate. The speaker is not really commenting on the recording in an objective way. He seems to view the recording as part of himself, not as something separate from himself which can be viewed from a purely external standpoint. His comments, then, are not comments on the recording, but comments which simply reveal part of his total view of himself. In the absence of any research designed to establish precisely what these comments do mean, since they seem unrelated to the recording, it is sufficient for us to conclude that for personal use the tape recorder has very limited application.

There are two further limitations that we need to consider, both elementary but both important. In the first place, the use of the apparatus demands some skill. This skill is quickly acquired and retained provided the machine is used frequently. Failure to operate the machine with a certain skill can result in a total failure to record or play-back. Skill is also required in using the microphone. To get satisfactory results, it is necessary to do a good deal more than merely speak into it or near it. In the second place, the fact that play-back requires as much time as the recording it reproduces, means that in a forty-minute lesson only twenty minutes are available for the actual practice of speech.

Advantages

Despite its considerable limitations, recording apparatus has certain distinct advantages. Speech, like music and theatre, is dynamic in essence. When it has been spoken it has gone beyond recall. It can be repeated, but the repeat is not the same as the original. It will have changed to some extent by the very act of repetition. Whereas we can recall the written words of Shakespeare by opening a book, we cannot recall the original performances. They have gone forever. The tape recorder can do something to overcome this. It will not, as we have seen, record the total speech act, but that part of it that it is able to record can be preserved indefinitely. We can play it again tomorrow and again next year.

Unlike the average camera, the tape recorder will reproduce what it has recorded as soon as the act of recording is finished. There is no waiting for the tape to be processed. This, too, is a considerable advantage. It means that we can play-back the sound made by a speaker whilst the image of his live performance is still fresh in our minds. The two are sufficiently closely related in time for us to be able to make comparisons between the recording and the reality.

Certain aspects of the total speech act can be reproduced with considerable fidelity by good recording apparatus. It will, for example, reproduce the words that are being used. 'Good morning, sir,' is not so distorted on reproduction as to be unrecognizable. Nor is it changed to 'Good afternoon, madam'. The phonetic aspects of speech are reproduced accurately. 'Ah' remains 'Ah'; it does not change on play-back to 'Oo'. If a speaker has a pronunciation characteristic of Hampshire, the apparatus will reproduce that pronunciation faithfully. This point is important since it may give rise to difficulties in the use of the apparatus in class. No purpose is served by using the apparatus at all unless the child whose speech is being played-back can believe in the ability of the apparatus to do its job. Since the speech issuing from the machine is entirely different from the concept of his speech that he carries in his head, it is not surprising that his first reaction should be to question the competence of the machine. To overcome this difficulty, it will frequently be necessary to refer to the rest of class. 'Is this a good reproduction of William's speech?' we might ask. The answer we want, of course, is an unequivocal, 'Yes'.

The Use of Recording Apparatus
Focus of Attention

Perhaps the most useful function of the tape recorder is to act as a focus of attention. Speech work which might seem a little unreal can be given an apparent significance by the use of the recorder. Suppose we wish to give a child an opportunity to explain himself orally at some length. We might decide to do this by using an interview situation. We could take four children whom we know to have interesting hobbies: one collects butterflies, the second breeds pigeons, the third is active in the Scout movement and the fourth trains with the local professional football team. To ask each in turn to speak to the class about his particular interest, might be demanding too much of them at this particular stage of their speech development. On the other hand, to have them interviewed by another member of the class whilst the rest of the class listens, might seem somewhat unreal. But if we told them that a team from the B.B.C. was in the district, collecting interesting local material for a sound radio programme, then by using recording apparatus we could give a certain point to the exercise. We could set the microphone in the middle of the table at which the four of them were seated with the interviewer, and we could tell the rest of the class that they were members of an invited audience who were expected to react carefully to the remarks made by the interviewees. Under the guise of 'rehearsing for the programme', we could give the interviewer and the interviewees considerable opportunities for practising their material. Despite the fact that this is ostensibly for a radio programme, we should ask for comments from the class on the achievement of the speakers before we let them hear the play-back, because we are concerned here with their total skill as speakers, not simply with their skill as sound broadcasters.

If we think it valuable to give more significance to the exercise, we can organize production teams that will in the course of time conduct a taped interview with everyone in the class. These interviews will be edited and arranged in a coherent order. Linking passages will be prepared and recorded. Finally, the completed tape can be played to the class, and their comments invited on its success as a piece of radio work.

The machine can be used in connection with the Outside Interview. With the permission of the interviewee, it can be used to record the statements made by both interviewer and interviewee. This leaves an inexperienced interviewer free to concentrate all his attention on getting the information he requires from the interviewee, instead of trying to write down that information during the course of the interview. A machine for this purpose will, of course, need to be easy to carry and independent of a mains power supply.

Occasionally the machine is of use in creating a focus of attention for dramatic work. A scene between two or three people that arises in the course of the drama class, can be developed and rehearsed in the presence of a microphone. Such detailed work with a small group of people in the presence of an inactive class, becomes easier to handle when it is being apparently conducted for the purpose of producing a perfect recording.

The value of the machine for all these purposes is that it allows practice in speech to be conducted. Its value arises from the practice itself, not from the fact that it will record and play-back the results of that practice.

Training the Listener

Speech, as we have seen, requires a listener, and a listener is also someone who is about to become a speaker; we might even define him as a speaker who for the moment is not speaking. What he hears as a listener will affect what he says as a speaker. The tape recorder can be useful in training the listener to listen.

Inevitably, when we record the speech of individuals in a class, the whole class will listen to the play-back. But we are restricted in how far we can use this fact to develop listening ability, by a consideration for the child who made the recording. It will not help him to have his speech minutely dissected in front of his contemporaries. What we need to do is to use speech for this purpose which is not connected with any member of the class. There are two ways in which we might do this:

i   To use our own speech to illustrate a particular point.
ii   To use the speech of others who have no connection with the class.

For both these approaches recording apparatus can be very useful.

i   *Our Own Speech*

The virtue of using our own speech as a basis for listening, is that we can highlight one aspect of speech at a time. The speech of a particular politician, for example, may be very quiet and very imprecisely articulated; the politician may have a marked local pronunciation which an inexperienced listener might confuse with articulatory imprecision; the arguments behind the speech may be confused; the quality of his voice may be nasal. All this constitutes too complex a pattern of sound to be useful as an initial approach to training in critical listening. By making demonstration tapes of our own speech, we can present the listening class with only one aspect at a time.

For example, to demonstrate the importance of adequate volume, we can make a range of recordings varying from absolute silence to extreme noise. We can ask the class to define the point at which the volume is correctly geared to the situation. We can do the same as far as articulation goes, beginning with a recording of speech that is so imprecisely articulated that it is totally incomprehensible, and moving in stages to the point where articulatory precision is so marked that it draws attention to itself to the detriment of what is being said. We can demonstrate what we mean by voice quality, by making recordings that range from very resonant to a lack of adequate resonance, from nasal to non-nasal. We can demonstrate the effect of excessive speed on the listener by recording at great speed a passage full of facts, and then asking the class to write down as many of these facts as it can remember. We can demonstrate a range of pitch variations from the point of no variation at all to the point where the variation is so considerable that it is out of keeping with the material that is being spoken. We can demonstrate inadequate organization of ideas. We can demonstrate, through varying types of speech, the varying impressions that a listener forms of the personality of the speaker.

ii *The Speech of Others*

Our own demonstrations will have provided a framework for the assessment of 'authentic' speech, speech which is designed for some other purpose than as a model for the class to dissect. We can build a collection of examples from many sources, but undoubtedly the best source is the radio.[1] From it we can collect a very wide range of examples—the interview with the man-in-the-street, the professional newsreader, the formal talk by a specialist—and comments on them can be as stringent and detailed as we wish, without causing offence to anyone. Examples that would be worth collecting for discussion with the class, might be these:

i   A cricket match commentary.

ii   A football match commentary.

iii   A boxing match commentary.

iv   A racing commentary.

v   The professional newsreaders. All radio newsreaders are doing the same job—reading printed facts in as unemotional a way as possible. Yet the speech of one such reader differs from that of another. We might make a useful comparison of these differences.

[1] The question of copyright is involved here. The *Annual Programme of Sound and Television Broadcasts to Schools and Colleges* contains a statement of the position, as far as the B.B.C. is concerned:

'As a general rule B.B.C. broadcasts may not be recorded without the permission of the B.B.C., the owners of the copyright in any musical or literary material and gramophone records used in the broadcasts and any dramatic or musical performers taking part in them. An exception to the general rule now exists in the case of B.B.C. school broadcasts under Section 41 of the Copyright Act of 1956 supplemented by arrangements which the B.B.C. has made with the interests concerned.

'Records of B.B.C. school broadcasts may therefore be made by schools without obtaining the above permissions provided that the records are only used for instructional purposes in class and that they are destroyed at the end of the school year.'

vi   Interviews with inexperienced broadcasters.

vii   A broadcast on behalf of a political party.

viii   The Christmas broadcast by Her Majesty The Queen. We may view the use of such a recording with some trepidation, but it would at least give us an opportunity to define the phrase, 'The Queen's English', and see how far that definition differed from the English used by The Queen.

ix   Speakers from different parts of the country. We could use such recordings in our discussions on how far pronunciation from different localities affected communication.

Radio is conceived in terms of sound. By contrast, television is conceived in terms of both sound and vision. It would be useful to record on tape a number of television broadcasts which are comparable with radio broadcasts in some way.[1] Television news broadcasts, cricket commentaries, and political broadcasts, are examples. It would then be possible for the class to make an assessment of how significant a part the visual is of the total speech act. This is important if we wish to avoid giving a child the impression that speech is something perceived solely in terms of sound.

To provide the class with a tangible framework within which to listen and make judgments on what it hears, we can employ an assessment scheme. Details of the form that such a scheme might take are considered in the next chapter.

Tape and the Teacher

Use can be made of recording apparatus for purposes which are of more direct value to the teacher than to the class. For example, it is difficult to remember at the end of a year what a child's speech was like at the beginning. In consequence, it is difficult to assess the degree of his development. By preserving a tape made of him at the beginning of the year, we have a point of reference. If there has been a development in those aspects of his speech that can be reproduced by a recorder, then it is likely that there has been a total development.

[1] Copyright applies here too. Permission to record must be sought from the broadcasting company concerned.

We can use the tape recorder to back up our comments on the speech of an individual child with whom we are doing work. Suppose we are working with Jennifer who is fourteen. When she speaks in anything but the most intimate of conversational situations, she is difficult to understand because of a marked articulatory imprecision. We would like her to do something about this, but we realize that we cannot hope for her to do so until she is convinced that some problem exists. This is the approach that we might employ:

TEACHER: I find you a bit difficult to understand, Jennifer. I can't really tell the difference between one word and another: you know what I mean?

JENNIFER: Mm . . . I think so. (*She is obviously confused.*)

TEACHER: Look; I've a recording here of somebody with the same difficulty. Listen to this. . . . (*We play a tape from our collection of examples; it is of ourself demonstrating imprecise articulation.*) Well—what about that?

JENNIFER: I can't understand it.

TEACHER: Nor can I. Can you *hear* him?

JENNIFER: Yes.

TEACHER: Well, if you can hear him, why can't you understand him?

JENNIFER: It's the words. I can't tell what he's talking about.

TEACHER: Look, Jennifer. Suppose you were in my position and he was sitting where you are—what would you say to him?

JENNIFER: Well—I'd tell him to open his mouth more.

TEACHER: You're quite right—that's part of it. But there's something else—I mean, listen. (*We open and close our mouth whilst making a noise, but we avoid making any movements of the tongue.*) That's not much better, is it? There's something else you'd have to tell him. Do you know what it is?

JENNIFER: To move his tongue?

TEACHER: That's it. Then you'll get something like this. (*We produce a quite clear statement which demonstrates use of jaw, lips and tongue.*) There you are. Now then, can you try it?

Jennifer speaks exactly as she did before. It is not that she has no clearer view of what imprecise articulation sounds like and what might be done to overcome the difficulty; it is simply that she does not see how all this applies to her. She has built up a concept of her own voice and speech over a period of fourteen years. The concept is, in consequence, a strong one. She can hear her own voice in her head, and since what she hears fits in with the concept, she concludes that our comments are unjustified. They arise, she may think, because we are unnecessarily finicky, or because we are judging her speech against quite unreal standards. She genuinely does not believe us when we say we are having difficulty in understanding her. This is quite reasonable. She is faced with the clear-cut choice of believing us and throwing overboard in a moment the clear view of her own speech that she has held for years, or of hanging on to that view and believing that we must be mistaken. In this sense, the problem is not one of increasing the precision of articulatory movement, but of changing the concept that Jennifer holds of her own speech. It is at this point that we might use the tape recorder:

TEACHER: I'll just switch this machine on, and then we can both hear what we sound like. . . . Now, I'm going to ask you where you're going for your holidays this year, but before I do let me tell you where I'm going. I'm going to a little place, etc. (*We make a statement about our forthcoming holidays. We do so because we want enough of our speech available on play-back for Jennifer to have to admit that the machine will reproduce speech faithfully.*) . . . Well then; and where are you going?

JENNIFER: The seaside.

TEACHER: Really. Whereabouts?

JENNIFER: Scarborough.

TEACHER: Have you been before?

JENNIFER: Last year—we went there last year.

TEACHER: What kind of things did you do?

JENNIFER: We went in the sea—played on the sands. . . . And my father took us—me and my brother—on a boat that goes to Filey. My father fished, but he didn't catch anything. My brother was just sick. . . .

TEACHER: Who was?

JENNIFER: My brother.

Our use of the tape for the purpose of backing up our view of Jennifer's speech, might sound like this:

TEACHER: Now let's play that back. . . .

MACHINE: Now, I'm going to ask you where you're going for your holidays this year, but before I do let me tell you where I'm going. I'm going to a little place in the Lake District called Patterdale. . . .

TEACHER: We'll stop it there for a moment. Now who's that talking?

JENNIFER: You, sir.

TEACHER: How do you know?

JENNIFER: Well, I recognize your voice and I remember you saying that.

TEACHER: Let's play some more.

MACHINE: . . . Well then; and where are you going? The seaside. Really. Whereabouts? Scarborough. Have you been before? Last year—we went there last year. What kind of things did you do?

TEACHER: That was me as well, wasn't it?

JENNIFER: Yes.

TEACHER: Who's the other speaker?

JENNIFER: Me.

TEACHER: How do you know?

JENNIFER: That's what I said—about going to Scarborough and having been there last year.

TEACHER: Good. Let's play the rest.

MACHINE: We went in the sea—played on the sands. . . . And my father took us—me and my brother—on a boat that goes to Filey. My father fished, but he didn't catch anything. My brother was just sick. . . . Who was? My brother.

TEACHER: Why do you think I said, 'Who was?'

JENNIFER: You didn't understand what I said first time.

TEACHER: Did you?

JENNIFER: It sounded like 'mother', then I remembered I'd said 'brother'.

Whereas it may not be too difficult for Jennifer to disregard our comment when it is in conflict with the concept she holds of her speech, it becomes a good deal more difficult when she is confronted by teacher plus machine.

Other Mechanical Aids

Three other pieces of apparatus might occasionally be used in connection with the development of speech.

i   Record Player

The Record Player can be used in connection with the training of the listener. It is, of course, restricted to the kind of records that are commercially available, and these records only rarely demonstrate the kind of things that we wish the class to listen to. Records of poetry speaking might be useful in introducing the class to the possibilities of interpretative speaking, but they should not be used so frequently that the class comes to regard such speaking as something that only other people do. They should follow up a listening period with a period in which they put into practice what they have learnt by listening. Commercial records of dramatic scenes exist; again, they are best used to further the class's own dramatic work. Recordings of both poetry and drama are at best recordings of only part of the total speech process.

ii   The Radio

The radio, as we have seen, can be a valuable source for tape-recorded material. The great virtue of the recorder is that it will preserve material for repeated play-back. But in a sense this destroys that material as speech, since speech is dynamic in essence. It is part of its nature that it cannot be recalled. The radio broadcast, used directly instead of through the tape recorder, might occasionally be of value as part of a listening programme. There is more pressure on the listener to take in

147

information first time, when he realizes that there is no possibility of hearing that material again.

iii *Television*

An increasing number of schools possess television sets and use them for educational purposes. A broadcasting company, putting out a programme on the earthworm clearly does not do so to further a speech course. But there may be value in considering the use of educational broadcasts as part of listener training. Television has the advantage over radio that it is concerned not only with the sound aspects of communication, but also with the visual.

5

Assessment Schemes

There will be times when we wish to make an assessment of the child's speech. We may wish to do this when we first meet him, so that we can see what his needs are. We may wish to do it, too, during the course of the next speech work we do with him, to measure the extent of his development.

Initial Assessment Scheme for the Teacher

For our initial assessment of a child's speech ability, we will need a fairly full scheme. This scheme should give us a picture of the child's total communication skill in a particular situation, and indicate the kind of work that is likely to be of particular benefit to him.

Whatever method we employ for making the assessment—reading aloud is probably the simplest—it must be one that allows some continuous speech from the child. We may use a 'tick-off' method of assessment with the scheme below: that is, we tick through the word or phrase that seems most appropriate. Ticks appearing on the left-hand side of the scheme indicate inadequacies; ticks on the right-hand side indicate satisfactoriness.

VOLUME:	Too quiet	Too loud	Satisfactory
ARTICULATION:	Imprecise	Too precise	Satisfactory
PITCH VARIATION:	Insufficient	Excessive	Satisfactory
SPEED:	Too fast	Too slow	Satisfactory
PRONUNCIATION:	Very markedly local	—	Satisfactory
VOICE QUALITY:	Strained	—	Easy

DEGREE OF NERVOUSNESS:	Considerable	Average	Little
CONTACT WITH LISTENER:	None	Fair	Good
ORGANIZATION OF MATERIAL:	Poor	Fair	Good
APPRECIATION OF SITUATION:	Poor	Fair	Good
FLUENCY:	Non-fluent	Fair	Good
VISUAL:	Little	Excessive	Satisfactory

DEFECTS NEEDING SPECIALIST ATTENTION:

>Lisp
>Stammer
>Excessive nasality
>Defective sounds—e.g. s, r, th
>Deafness.

CHILD'S PARTICULAR NEEDS:

OVERALL GRADING: A B C // D

Running Assessments

These might be employed to make an assessment of the child after every piece of work. They should be much briefer than the full scheme. They should give an indication of week-to-week progress.

EXERCISE:

TECHNICAL DIFFICULTIES: (volume, articulation, etc.)

ORGANIZATIONAL DIFFICULTIES: (Muddled, illogical, etc.)

PROGRESS: (a little louder this time, etc.)

PARTICULAR POINTS THAT NEED ATTENTION: (still more work on volume, etc.)

GRADE FOR THIS EXERCISE: A B C // D

Schemes for the Class

One of the difficulties of working in class with the individual reader, or with the small interview situation, is to find some way of involving the whole class in the work. The use of some simple assessment scheme by the listeners, is one way in which we might help to achieve this involvement. But such an approach has other virtues: it directs the listening of the class into certain channels; it gives them a framework of reference; it helps to restrict comments to those which are useful.

ASSESSMENT OF PARTICULAR SITUATIONS (e.g. the 'panel' situation).

COULD I HEAR HIM?

> Yes
> Not very well
> No

COULD I UNDERSTAND HIM?

> Yes
> Not very well
> No

WAS HE TALKING TO US?

> Yes
> Some of the time
> No

WHAT WAS HE TRYING TO DO? (e.g. to get me to travel by train instead of by bus.)

DID HE SUCCEED?

> Very well
> Fairly well
> No

WHAT POINTS DOES HE NEED TO WATCH IN PARTICULAR? (e.g. he needs to talk *to* us more.)

More complex forms of assessment can be evolved as the class becomes more sophisticated in listening to the work of its members. They should not become so complex that the information they provide is so detailed that it is no longer useful to the speaker. They can, however, be more complex when the speaker is not one of the class, and the intention is to encourage critical listening for its own sake. For example, in the case of the class listening to a speaker on television, an assessment scheme on these lines might be used:

Scheme for Critical Listening

COULD I HEAR HIM?

> Yes
> Not very well
> No

COULD I UNDERSTAND HIM?

> Yes
> Not very well
> No

WHO WAS HE TALKING TO? (e.g. an interviewer, the viewers.)

DID HE ESTABLISH A GOOD CONTACT WITH THE LISTENER (S)?

> Yes
> Fairly good
> No

WHAT DID I THINK OF THE SPEED?

> Just right
> Too slow
> Too fast

WAS HE INTERESTED IN WHAT HE WAS SAYING?

> Yes
> Perhaps
> No

DID HE COMMUNICATE VISUALLY?

> Yes
> Partly
> No

WHAT WAS HE TRYING TO TELL ME? (e.g. the kind of things I would see if I went to Israel.)

DID HE SUCCEED?

> Very well
> Fairly well
> No

WHAT SHOULD HE DO TO IMPROVE HIS NEXT TELEVISION APPEAR-
ANCE? (e.g. prepare his material better, speak more slowly.)
WHAT GRADE WOULD I GIVE HIM OUT OF THESE?

A B C // D

School Tests in Speech

These are two possible tests which we might find it useful to conduct at the end of each year. One is conducted by the teacher with the individual child; the other is conducted with the participation of the class.

The Individual Test

A useful and well-tried test for making an assessment of the child's speech ability, is the two-part 'live' test. Part 1 of the test consists of asking the child to read to us a passage of prose from a distance of ten to fifteen feet. The passage will have been selected for its readability rather than its literary value. The child will have been allowed to prepare it for about ten minutes. Part 2 of the test consists of what we might call 'a conversation' between ourselves and the child. These are the points we will need to assess in Part 1 of the test:

i *The child's speech in general*

We will have to take into account such factors as Audibility and Intelligibility, Speed and Fluency. Voice quality will have to be noted inasmuch as it is part of the total communicative act. We will note word-stress where it differs markedly from common usage.

ii *Interpretation*

We will have to decide to what extent the child has

succeeded in grasping the total intention of the author, and then managed to convey that meaning to us. We will have to decide to what extent the child has succeeded in conveying to us the nature of any characters involved in the passage.

iii *Communication*

We will have to decide the extent to which the child has established a relationship with us as listeners and how far he has succeeded in maintaining that relationship throughout the reading.

On the basis of our decisions under these three headings, we can give a grade on the four-point scale of A B C // D. These are the points we will need to assess in Part 2 of the test:

i *The child's speech in conversation*

Does he maintain reasonable standards of speech in this situation? Is he still entirely audible and intelligible?

ii *His use of language*

Having decided what he is going to say, has the child the ability to organize it and express it in appropriate language? Is he fluent or halting in his use of language?

iii *Communication*

What degree of contact does the child establish with us as listeners? Does he maintain that contact throughout the conversation? Does he understand the nature of the situation, or does he keep us in the position of interrogators to whose questions he gives brief and undeveloped answers?

Again, we can give him a general mark for his ability in this part of the test, on the basis of the four-point scale: A B C // D.

The Class Test

Provided the child has been through some coherent speech education process in class, there are points in favour of the Class Test, so long as we make sure that it is properly controlled. In the first place, it can be conducted during the last speech periods of the term so that no disruption of the school organization takes place. In the second place, it is conducted in a situation that the child has been experiencing throughout the term.

154

In the third place, it has an educational as well as a testing value in that the class is still expected to listen and evaluate, and the speaker is still expected to communicate to it.

There are many forms that such a test might take. We might, for example, decide that the child should read a prepared passage to the class, and then be interviewed by two or three of his contemporaries on a topic of his own choice. We might decide that, since we have not used the reading approach to speech work during the term, it would be better if he made a prepared statement to the class and then faced questions on it. Whatever form we decided to use would need to be worked out in some detail, together with an appropriate assessment scheme to be used by the class.

External Tests in Speech

External tests in speech seem likely to affect schools more and more. Three university examining boards for the General Certificate of Education already conduct such tests. All are two-part 'live' tests, on the lines of that described earlier. The work of Dr Hitchman in the University of Nottingham has established the degree of reliability of such tests.

The Joint Matriculation Board of the Northern Universities introduced an optional test in 1954. This has now become an established optional test tied to the written paper in General Studies at Advanced level. The number of candidates, though still very small (under 800 in 1963), continues to rise steadily.

The School Examination Board of the University of Durham, introduced a test in 1957. This was an optional non-G.C.E. test, designed for candidates in the 15 – 16+ age-range. It was not tied to any written paper. In 1964 it involved about 800 candidates. An interesting feature of this test, which came to an end in 1964 when the Durham Board closed, was that about 50 per cent of the candidates were from non-Grammar schools. In a sense, then, this test could be regarded as a useful experiment in connection with the Certificate of Secondary Education.

The School Examinations Council of the University of London, introduced a test in 1964. This was an optional test, tied to the written paper in English Language at the Ordinary level. In its first year it dealt with some 16,000 candidates.

The Examining Boards of the Universities of Oxford and Cambridge are preparing to introduce their own tests. It seems likely that other established Boards will consider doing so in the future.

Many experiments have been conducted in various parts of the country, in connection with the testing of spoken English as part of the Certificate of Secondary Education. In some areas there has been an understandable caution about establishing at once, compulsory tests in the subject, but this caution is by no means universal. To judge from the feeling of many schools, whatever the form of test finally decided upon, the regular testing of speech in schools is likely to become a permanent feature of the British educational scene in the future.

Further Reading

AIKIN, W. A. *The Voice.* Longmans.

DEWEY, J. *How We Think.* Heath.

EDFELDT, A. W. *Silent Speech and Silent Reading.* Almqvist and Wiksell, Stockholm.

EWING, I. R. and EWING, A. W. G. *The Handicap of Deafness.* Longmans.

GREENE, M. C. L. *Learning to Talk.* Heinemann.

LEWIS, M. M. *Infant Speech.* Routledge and Kegan Paul.

LURIA, A. R. and YUDOVITCH, F. I. *Speech and the Development of Mental Processes in the Child.* Staples.

MACARTHY, P. A. D. *An English Pronouncing Vocabulary.* Heffer.

PIAGET, J. *The Language and Thought of the Child.* Routledge and Kegan Paul.

PIAGET, J. *The Child's Conception of the World.* Routledge and Kegan Paul.

STANISLAVSKY, K. *An Actor Prepares.* Bles.

VYGOTSKY, L. S. *Thought and Language.* The M.I.T. Press and John Wiley and Sons.

WATTS, A. F. *The Language and Mental Development of Children.* Harrap.

WISE, A. *Reading and Talking in English.* Harrap.